Faith
Development
and
Pastoral Care

THEOLOGY AND PASTORAL CARE SERIES

edited by
Don S. Browning

Ritual and Pastoral Care
by Elaine Ramshaw

Faith Development and Pastoral Care
by James S. Fowler

JAMES W. FOWLER

Faith Development and Pastoral Care

Don S. Browning, *editor*

THEOLOGY AND PASTORAL CARE

FORTRESS PRESS
PHILADELPHIA

Library of Congress Cataloging-in-Publication Data
Fowler, James W., 1940–
    Faith development and pastoral care.
    (Theology and pastoral care series)
    Bibliography: p.
    1. Pastoral theology. 2. Faith. 3. Developmental psychology. I. Title. II. Series.
    BV4011.6.F69   1986   253   86-45904
    ISBN 0-8006-1739-8

Printed in the U.S.A.   1-1739

11   12   13   14   15   16

To
Jim L. Waits
and
James T. Laney
leaders linking university and church

Contents

Series Foreword

Our purpose in the Theology and Pastoral Care Series is to present ministers and church leaders with a series of readable books that will (1) retrieve the theological and ethical foundations of the Judeo-Christian tradition for pastoral care, (2) develop lines of communication between pastoral theology and the other disciplines of theology, (3) create an ecumenical dialogue on pastoral care, and (4) do this in such a way as to affirm yet go beyond the recent preoccupation of pastoral care with secular psychotherapy and the other social sciences.

The books in this series are written by authors who are well acquainted with psychology, psychotherapy, and the other social sciences. All of the authors affirm the importance of these disciplines for modern societies and for ministry in particular, but they see them also as potentially destructive of human values unless they are guided in their practical application by tested religious and ethical traditions. But to retrieve the best of the Judeo-Christian tradition for the church's care and counseling is a challenging intellectual task—a task to which few writers in the area of pastoral care have attended with sufficient thoroughness. This series addresses that task out of a broad ecumenical stance, with all of the authors taking an ecumenical approach to theology. Besides a vigorous investigation of Protestant resources, there are specific treatments of pastoral care in Judaism and Catholicism.

We hope that the series will help ministers and church leaders view afresh the theological and ethical foundations of care and counseling. All of the books have a practical dimension, but even more important than that, they help us see care and counseling differently. Compared with writings of the last thirty years in this field, some of the books will seem startlingly different. They will need to be read and pondered with care. But I have little doubt that the series will make a profound and lasting impact upon the way we understand and practice our care for one another.

James Fowler needs little introduction to the likely readers of this book. He is widely known as the author and developer of faith-development research. His *Stages of Faith* (1981) is one of the most widely read books in contemporary religious publishing. His work has been most immediately relevant to religious education. But it has been used as well in a variety of other practical contexts. Pastoral care and pastoral counseling also have turned to Fowler's theory of the stages of faith development to clarify and guide the work of these ministries. Until recently, the relevance of faith-development theory to pastoral care has been a subject of speculation by others. Now, in *Faith Development and Pastoral Care,* James Fowler has given us his own interpretation of the relevance to pastoral care of his important research on how faith develops.

For over fifteen years, first at Harvard University and Boston College, and now at Emory University as the Director of the Center for Faith Development, James Fowler has been reworking the structuralism of Jean Piaget, the psychology of Erik Erikson, and the phenomenologies of faith of H. R. Niebuhr and Paul Tillich to clarify our understanding of the development of faith. Faith, as Fowler uses the concept, is understood primarily as a particular way of knowing and valuing. In the present volume, however, we witness a broadening of the thinking begun in his *Becoming Adult, Becoming Christian* (1984). As in that work, Fowler here synthesizes his faith-development theory with a theory of Christian vocation and an understanding of the importance of narrative for the communication of specifically Christian understandings of character.

In *Faith Development and Pastoral Care,* Fowler carries these themes further. But we have in this important work several firsts that will both intrigue Fowler watchers and make substantive contributions to pastoral care. First, he places pastoral care firmly within the emerging discipline of practical theology by discussing what he calls a "practical theology of pastoral care." Second, he does this for a particular understanding of the church that he calls the "public church." Third, he advances a broad understanding of pastoral care as forming lives within the church for the purposes of Christian vocation in the world. Fourth, he extends his theory of faith development by relating it to Robert Kegan's theory of the "evolving self." This is particularly useful for the purpose of relating faith development to the intimacies of the development of the self encountered and fostered in pastoral care. Fifth, he applies his theory of faith development not only to individuals in their pilgrimage toward Christian vocation but also to the assessment of the stages of development of what he calls various "congregational presences." And finally, the book ends on a stunningly practical note with the introduction of the "tapestry of life" survey, which will prove to be a useful guide for deepening both pastoral care and religious education.

In short, we do not find a warmed-over summary of faith-development theory in this book; instead, we find a bold extension of it into a new arena of practical theology that will greatly benefit concrete practice in the areas of pastoral care and counseling.

CHAPTER 1

Toward a Practical
Theology
of Pastoral Care

NEW LIFE FOR PRACTICAL
THEOLOGY

We find ourselves in the midst of a quiet but deep-going revolution in the relationship of theological education to the church and its ministries. This revolution centers in the recovery of practical theology as a discipline. It has not been too long since practical theology was regarded as a basement operation in most divinity schools and theological seminaries. And I mean that literally: departments of pastoral care, Christian education, church administration, and homiletics frequently were actually located in basements, added as though they were afterthoughts—which in fact they often were. You could almost count on it: the more academically prestigious the school of theology, the greater the status difference between the so-called classical disciplines of biblical studies, church history, systematic theology, and ethics, on the one hand, and the so-called applied disciplines, on the other.

That older arrangement of the division of labor in theological education rested upon an unfortunate understanding of the relation between theory and practice. In an interesting series of historical turns, which Edward Farley[1] has effectively traced for us, we can see four major phases through which theology came to be divided along the lines of the theoretical and the applied. In the first phase, which began with the New Testament era and continued until the early Middle Ages, theology amounted to personal and existential inquiry into the mysteries of divine revelation undertaken for the sake of helping the Christian community live toward truth. Farley calls this approach to theology *theology habitus*—theology as knowledge of God pursued through disciplines of prayer, study, and liturgical participation and aimed toward the formation of persons and community in accordance with the knowledge of God.

The second phase began with the intellectual responses of the church to the challenges of heresies within and competitive intellectual ideologies from without. It culminated in the intellectual synthesis of Thomas Aquinas in the High Middle Ages. Farley calls this second phase *theology science*. In this era theology constituted the ordering framework for grounding all human knowledge. Theology science provided the intellectual energy and thrust for the founding of the great medieval universities, and persisted—at least in Roman Catholicism—until well beyond the Counter-Reformation.

The next great wave of change in theology came from within those early European universities, or their descendants: first there came the impact of the Renaissance and the Reformation, with their respective returns to classical and biblical antiquity. Then came the Enlightenment's spirit of rational inquiry, with its emerging methods of critical, scientific empirical study. No longer "queen of the sciences," theology had to struggle to maintain a presence in the transformed universities. By forming alliances with the emerging "scientific" disciplines of history, linguistics, epistemology, and rationally grounded ethics, various departments of specialized theological study began to form. *Theology science* became *theological sciences*. A unity and working relation between these disciplinary specialties in theology derived from their contributions to the professional grounding of university-educated pastors. But each discipline developed a primary loyalty to the secular field from which it drew its methods and legitimacy. And as specialization continued, professional guilds of scholars in the various theological disciplines generated both confidence and isolation from one another through the evolution of highly differentiated and technical methods and nomenclatures.

Finally, in a phase that has been dominant from the late nineteenth century until recently, theology has primarily meant the enterprise called *systematic* or *dogmatic theology*, with fields like fundamental and philosophical theology serving as specialties within the larger field of dogmatics.

In the development characterized by these four phases we see how theology has come to be a specialized academic enterprise modeled to a significant degree on the ideal of pure theoretical inquiry. Practical theology, in relation to this ideal, came to be understood as applied theology—the adaptation and application of truths generated in pure theological study and construction to the actual practical contexts and problems of ministry and the life of the church. In this view practical theology has come to be seen as a derivative of systematic theology and the other supporting theological disciplines. Its creativity has been understood to be limited to the translation of truths derived elsewhere and to the drawing of the implications of more scholarly work for the practical tasks of ministry.

The emerging new field of practical theology has directly challenged this state of affairs. It has forcefully reasserted that theology, in any "classical" era we know of, was eminently *practical* theology. It had more of the character of theology habitus than of the theological sciences. Moreover, the resurgence of practical theology has derived clarity and confidence about its purpose from the movement toward center in theology and philosophy of the ancient concept of *praxis*.

In the Greek city-state of which Aristotle wrote, the kind of knowing and ability required for the highest of Greek vocations—good political leadership—was that of *praxis*.[2] Capacity for leadership in the political *praxis* of the city-state required at least three elements: first, a grounding in the myths and history of the polis and in its evolved purposes and ideals, a grounding in the city-state's story and vision; second, a knowledge of human nature and of the arts of organization and persuasion involved in leadership; and third, a capacity for analyzing and understanding the factors shaping the present moment and their challenges to the welfare of the people. In *praxis* these elements or capacities of knowing find integration in a pattern in which action and ongoing reflection interpenetrate. The good politician manages to lead the people forward in the realization of the unique purposes of the community, through methods that take account of both the human "stuff" of which the people are made and the unique pattern of internal and external factors that threaten or challenge the mission of the polis. The kind of knowing that *praxis* requires is often taken as synonymous with *phronesis*, which translates as prudence—a practical wisdom that informs action.[3]

Aristotle contrasted the knowing underlying *praxis* with two other distinguishable kinds of knowing: *theoria* and *poeisis*.[4] *Theoria* is knowledge born of analytic distance and objectivity. In detached observation and analysis of the action in the Olympic games, "theorists" advised participants on how best to train and develop strategies for the competition. At another level, *theoria* was the fruit of philosophical reflection, resulting from the intellect's inspired contemplation on metaphysical reality.

Theoria, of course, stands behind our modern concept of theory. For our purposes it is important to see that *theoria* and *praxis* are not opposites. Nor is one the derivative of the other. They are richly complementary but distinct forms of knowing animated by different interests and contexts and employing different methods.

A third kind of knowing that Aristotle identified points to what we might call creative skill. This is *poeisis.* When a potter mixes clay to the right consistency, centers it on the wheel, and then gradually forms and lifts it into a graceful vase, she employs *poeisis.* The process of learning to ski or swim involves developing in the kind of knowing that is *poeisis.* Verbal or conceptual orientation simply is not adequate for this kind of learning; one must feel with one's body the coordination of limbs and sensory signals that makes these complex uses of self possible. In the work of ministry the gestures and action of sacramental leadership constitute one area in which the creative and artistic intuition and developed skills of *poeisis* make important contributions.

As we shall see in this book, *theoria* has an important set of contributions to make to the *praxis* of ministry and of congregational pastoral care. Of special interest will be the contribution that faith-development research and theory can make to pastoral care. Similarly, there are points at which the distinction between *praxis* and *poeisis* gets blurred and in which skills that qualify the self are essential to *praxis.* The formation of persons and community for pastoral care involves the development of skills and abilities, some of which have elements of *poeisis.* In the main, however, as a contribution to the practical theology of pastoral care, this book focuses on that kind of knowing which informs *praxis.* We are concerned with how pastoral leaders can effectively lead in the formation of the congregation as an ecology of care in the challenges of *this present world,* for the sake of fulfilling the mission of the community of Christian faith.

When we take *praxis* seriously as the basic concern of practical theology, we need to bear in mind an essential duality in its meaning:[5] *praxis* is both customary and transformative. On the one hand, it involves the ways in which things get done in a community. It comprises the ways in which a community does its business—the patterns of action and transaction that constitute its accustomed ways of doing things. On the other hand, *praxis* involves strategic initiatives and intentional action aimed at the transformation of the community toward a more effective realization of its purposes and a more faithful alignment with its master story and vision. We can distinguish between these two senses of *praxis* by referring to them as respectively the maintenance and the transformative dimensions of *praxis*. Any adequate approach to a practical theology of pastoral care will have to concern itself with both dimensions.

THE DISCIPLINES AND STRUCTURE OF PRACTICAL THEOLOGY

Who does practical theology? My claim will be that the community of faith—the church—taken as a whole does. Both within the community and beyond its local circles, some persons, to be sure, take special responsibilities and bring special competences to the work of practical theology. But the work itself is theological inquiry and reflection undertaken in the midst of the church's ongoing life, for the guidance and direction of the community of faith in the interest of faithfulness and effectiveness in the conduct of its mission. To modify and extend a characterization I first offered several years ago, practical theology is

> theological reflection and construction arising out of and giving guidance to a community of faith in the *praxis* of its mission. Practical theology is critical and constructive reflection leading to ongoing modification and development of the ways the church shapes its life to be in partnership with God's work in the world.[6]

The church does practical theology. Whether consciously and in a disciplined manner or unconsciously and haphazardly, it makes interpretations, decisions, and determinations that maintain, modify, or extend its *praxis*.

Perhaps a kind of flow chart that maps the sources and loci of practical theology and their interrelatedness can be of help. I offer two charts.[7] In the first of them (see fig. 1), we begin with a central focus on *ecclesial praxis*—the pattern of the church's efforts to be in partnership with God in the world and faithfully to carry out the dimensions of its mission. Those dimensions are taken as constitutive of *ecclesial praxis*. In *practical theology* the church's mission must constantly be seen and evaluated and must continually be reformed in the light of the *present situations and challenges* of the church's environment. At the same time, both *ecclesial praxis* and the *present situation and challenges* must be held up to the interpretive and normative light of Scripture and tradition—the church's story and vision. Notice

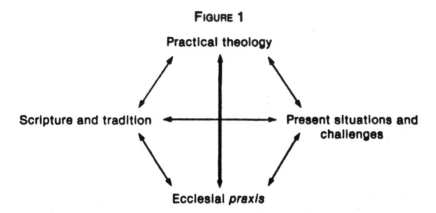

FIGURE 1

Proclamation: sacraments; care and cure
of souls; formation and transformation of
persons; social, economic, and political
engagement; administration; support of
lay vocations in the world

that the lines of communication, information flow, discernment, and impact are all two-directional. In *practical theology* the perception and interpretation of *present situations and challenges* reflects the shaping power of *Scripture and tradition*. Similarly, the questions put to *Scripture and tradition* continue to change and be enriched by the church's struggle to relate the dimensions of its mission to *present situations and challenges*. The work of *practical theology*, seeking to mediate the relation between *Scripture and tradition* and *present situations and challenges*, arises from and returns to *ecclesial praxis*. Theologian David Tracy has characterized the interplay between *Scripture and tradition* and *present situations and challenges* which practical theology seeks to mediate as an ongoing process of "mutually critical correlation."[8]

We began our charting of the sources and loci of practical theology with the central axis of *practical theology* and its action-reflection relation to *ecclesial praxis*. The full-orbed representation of its work, however, requires that we show the relation of *practical theology* to other of the theological and nontheological disciplines that help to inform it. Let us expand our chart (see fig. 2). Now we can see how the work of *practical theology*, as a concern of centers of theological research and education and of specialists who devote their main energies to some aspects of it, relates to other theological and

FIGURE 2

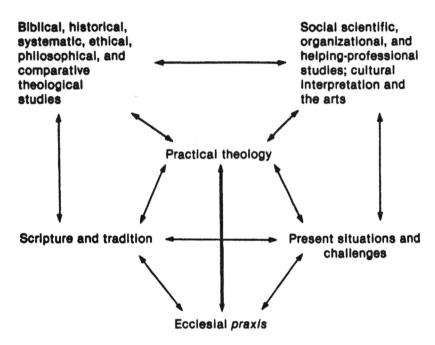

Biblical, historical, systematic, ethical, philosophical, and comparative theological studies

Social scientific, organizational, and helping-professional studies; cultural interpretation and the arts

Practical theology

Scripture and tradition

Present situations and challenges

Ecclesial *praxis*

Proclamation: sacraments; care and cure of souls; formation and transformation of persons; social, economic and political engagement; administration; support of lay vocations in the world

nontheological disciplines. *Practical theology*, working in the local church, the theological seminary, or the university divinity school, makes its own analyses of *Scripture and tradition*, on the one hand, and of *Present situations and challenges*, on the other. It recognizes, however, that there are highly developed specialities and methods—and bodies of literature and knowledge—that open up the depths and textures of both *Scripture and tradition* and *present situations and challenges*. Moreover, there are some theological disciplines—ethics, for example—that have made a specialty of relating the normative perspectives of Christian faith to situations of responsibility, choice, and action. Therefore, practical theological inquiry and reflection attend to the resources provided by both theological and nontheological disciplines which can deepen its penetration of its sources and challenges and help it avoid shallowness and superficiality in the directions it formulates. Theologically educated pastors and professors who concentrate on the interdisciplinary linkages of practical theology with cognate theological and nontheological fields have special contributions to make to the community of faith as it does its practical theological work. But it is of the essence of practical theology's integrity that it makes the axis of ecclesial *praxis* and practical theological reflection the center from which questions to the specialized theological and nontheological disciplines are shaped and to which they are kept accountable.

A PRACTICAL THEOLOGY OF PASTORAL CARE

This book focuses on a practical theology of pastoral care. This means that on the central axis of practical theological reflection and ecclesial *praxis* which we charted above, we will be attending primarily to action and reflection in two areas of the congregation's work: the care and cure of souls and the formation and transformation of persons. Ours will be an "ecological" approach to the congregation. My employment of the ecological metaphor runs in two directions. First, we will consider the community of faith as an "ecology of care." That is to say, in approaching a practical theology of pastoral care we will try to honor the richness of relationships in the interdependent community of the congregation. Some of the interdependence of congregations can be seen in the formal activities of a church: public worship, the governing boards, the men's and women's groups, Sunday-school classes, work areas, committees, youth groups, and the like. Much of the "thickness" or the redemptive toughness of congregations as ecologies of care, however, is not visible on organizational charts, in membership lists, or in the more or less formalized activities of the community. Cords of friendship, long histories of family interrelatedness, small prayer groups, frequent patterns of telephone conversations, spontaneous responses when there are emergencies or hard times, business interests fostered through weekly contact, and many other patterns of uniquely intimate interaction and reliance constitute important elements in the fibrous texture of congregational life. These, in addition to the more visible and formalized structures of church activity, constitute an ecology of care. In this book my concern is to offer an account of the animating and ordering purposes of congregational care and to draw on theological and social-scientific perspectives from faith development theory to frame approaches to making such care more consistent, intentional, and effective.

But there is a second use of the ecological metaphor we must attend to: we will consider the community of faith as an "ecology of vocation." Vocation, as we shall see in the next chapter, must not be reduced to occupation, profession, or career. It has to do with the response persons make to God's call to partnership and with the way that response exerts ordering power in a person or community's priorities and investments of self, time, and resources. In ways that parallel our earlier distinction between *praxis* as maintenance and *praxis* in the interest of transformation, the congregation can be seen as an ecology both of care and of transformation. A practical theology of pastoral care must embrace both.

In the next chapter I will set forth the outlines of an understanding of the purpose of the church as the nurturing and forming of men and women to respond in effective faithfulness to the call of God to partnership with God's work in the world. From this perspective, *pastoral care consists of all the ways a community of faith, under pastoral leadership, intentionally sponsors the awakening, shaping, rectifying, healing, and ongoing growth in vocation of Christian persons and community, under the pressure and power of the in-breaking kingdom of God.*

My approach to pastoral care is based on the conviction that the Christian faith offers us a determinant conception of the human vocation—the human calling or destiny. This I take to be the calling to partnership with God in God's work of ongoing creation, governance, redemption, and liberation. I speak here not of the idea of *Christian* vocation, as important as that undoubtedly is. Rather, I speak of the Christian understanding and interpretation of the *human* vocation. The approach to pastoral care that I offer finds its focal center, therefore, in the intentional efforts congregations make, with the leadership of pastoral practical theologians, to awaken and form persons for their vocations. This pattern of care—aimed both at maintenance and at ongoing transformation of the community— works at the rectification or correction of vocation, and at healing, redemption, and regeneration when vocation has been lost or forfeited. The pressure toward growth and continued sharpening of attentiveness in partnership comes from God's future, the kingdom of God—the commonwealth of love and justice—which God's work and our partnership aim at and anticipate.

In the view developed here we will underline the fact that pastors have unique roles to play in helping to form and maintain congregations as ecologies of care and vocation. We will emphasize that ordained ministers are called to provide the kind of leadership that contributes to growth in individual and communal commitments to congregational care. Søren Kierkegaard has instructed us to view the calling of the church in terms of a company of actors in a drama occurring before God, in the world. In Kierkegaard's figure[9] it is the task of the pastor as practical theologian to be the prompter for the drama. He or she is charged with being sure that the Christian actors in this worldly drama, played at high stakes before the Almighty One, get the "script" right. In proclamation and sacramental leadership and through teaching of many kinds, pastors are charged with getting the story and vision right and with forming the people as competent speakers and livers of the grammar of Christian faith. In pastoral care they call forth and help form skills and capacities in their members which strengthen the congregation as an ecology of care and as a spawning ground of vocation.

But we must not give the ironic Dane the last word on the pastor, with his image of the prompter. Kierkegaard brilliantly engages readers with his own parabolic vision through a maze of pseudonyms and alter-identities. In doing so he illustrates a stronger and more personal role for the pastoral theologian than our interpretations of his image of the prompter—as important as that is—might suggest. Charles Gerkin suggests that the pastoral leader in care and vocation must be a parabolic person. The parables of Jesus—and of Kierkegaard, who so aptly imitated them—have the effect of jarring the assumptive worlds of their hearers. They make the familiar strange and turn some part of one's taken-for-granted reality upside down in the interest of a crosscutting truth. The pastor, says Gerkin, through her or his embodiment and articulation of the story and vision and by hermeneutic skill in helping the power of the gospel meet and heal the broken stories of the congregation—and by virtue of the pastoral office—bears the burden and the joy of being a parabolic person.[10]

THE VOCATION OF A
PUBLIC CHURCH

In 1977 the brilliant young sociologist Richard Sennett published the book *The Fall of Public Man*.[11] Looking intently at the middle decades of the eighteenth, the nineteenth, and the twentieth centuries, he focused on three major cities, New York, London, and Paris, asking how the lines between the private and public aspects of our lives have changed over a two-hundred-year period. How, for instance, have the meaning and quality of persons' lives in public changed? What consequences flow from that change?

Sennett's complex argument, perhaps oversimply summarized, is that across two centuries we have seen a steady but dramatic shift in which public life has been emptied of much of its significance as an arena for general participation. Increasingly, public life has been left to the control of professional elites. Most members of society, intimidated by the bigness of our institutions and by the complexities of government, have settled for roles as spectators. The political process, now mediated to the public by mass telecommunications, is increasingly under the control of smaller and more insulated elites, with conventions and public debates falling into the category of entertainment for passive onlookers in the privacy of their homes.

Meanwhile, Sennett says, as participation in public life has diminished as an arena for the playing of meaningful roles, we moderns have placed more and more weight on the private domains of family, marriage, and intimate relations as the contexts where our life meanings are worked out. We have fallen, he suggests, into a kind of "tyranny of intimacy."[12] This gives rise to an expectation that the real satisfactions and fulfillments of our lives will come from our interpersonal relations. It encourages an attitude that work and interaction in public life are merely "roles we play" in order to secure, earn, and enjoy life in the private sphere. In our religion, in our membership in associations, and in our work, this analysis suggests, we are increasingly drawn (and restricted) to circles of persons like ourselves with whom we can hope to enjoy the emotional and relational closeness that makes for fulfilling intimacy.

Stirred by the work of Sennett and others, and concerned about the widespread privatization of church and religion in American life in the late seventies, several influential authors have begun to write and teach about the idea of a *public church*. The idea first came to my attention in the 1981 book by Martin E. Marty, *The Public Church*.[13] Later in the same year Parker J. Palmer made an important contribution to this kind of thinking with his book *The Company of Strangers*.[14] Both writers were to some extent influenced by the need for mainline Protestant and Catholic churches to recover initiatives in the face of the political emergence of the movements of a new religious right in the country. What is the vision of a public church that has taken form in Marty's and Palmer's work? From the richness and range of their books I would identify four central characteristics.

First, the public church is deeply and particularly Christian. Neither Marty nor Palmer advocates some sort of religion in general or homogenized brand of ecclesial life. A public church, in their sense of the term, is a worshiping community whose life is centered in God's self-revelation in Jesus Christ. In this respect and others, the public church is to be clearly distinguished from the idea of an American civil religion. It is a particular community of faith standing in the normativity of a religious tradition.

Second, it is a church committed to Jesus Christ, under the sovereignty of God, that is prepared to pursue its mission in the context of a pluralistic society. That is to say, it does not believe that the only faithful way to relate to its variety of Christian and non-Christian neighbors is through proselytization, on the one hand, or anathema and judgment, on the other. Such a church is prepared to give its witness and to invite the stranger to saving faith in Jesus Christ. But it is also willing to share its story and offer the wisdom of Christian faith to others in a spirit that intends relation and cooperation for the common good with those whose previous commitments and traditions do not make them candidates for conversion. A public church, therefore, is one that is faithful to its particularity and shares its central story but is prepared to join shoulder to shoulder with non-Christians in order to address and work redemptively at problems confronting or threatening the common good.

Third, a public church is one in which the encouragement of intimacy within its community and the concern for family feeling are balanced by care about the more impersonal and structural domains of public life. A public church encourages and supports its members in the development of vocations in which partnership with God is carried into the large-scale economic, technical, political, commercial, and religious structures that shape our lives. The public church blesses and strengthens persons for Christian presence in the ambiguities and amoralities of large-scale corporate and governmental processes. A public church frees its members from many of the tasks of institutional maintenance and internal ministry for the sake of strengthening their vocations as Christians in the marketplace, the school, the law office, the legislative halls, the hospital, and the councils of defense policy making.

Fourth, a public church is one unafraid of engagement with the complexities and ambiguities of thought and ideologies in this age of ideological pluralism. Convinced of the truth of its conviction of the sovereignty of God, the public church knows that God is greater and more than even our most adequate theologies can fully grasp. Therefore, it engages with others in confident openness, guided by the confidence that God often uses the truths of others to refine, reground, or correct our own. The public church is a nondefensive church: it does not have to coerce or control. It witnesses to the transcendent God whose self-disclosure is the center of our history—the hinge of history[13]—and who keeps coming to us from the future, expanding and correcting our grasp of the event of Christ and giving us eyes to see and nerve to respond to the in-breaking kingdom of God. In the service of this massive fact the public church can be a community of faith committed to civility—to a quality of rigorous but calm discussion of truth. It can be a witness that God's kingdom is not advanced by violence or by the tactics of ideological storm troopers even if they carry the sign of the cross.

In subsequent chapters as we look at the church as ecology of care and vocation, it is the public church we will have in view. Building on a theology of God's action and human partnership, we will in time come to a consideration of faith development theory as a framework for informing a practical theology of pastoral care in the development of a public church as an ecology of care and vocation. For now we turn to an examination of vocation and covenant community as foundational bases for a public church and its work in practical theology.

CHAPTER 2

A Community of Calling and Covenant

Our characterization of pastoral care has placed at center the calling and fitting of persons for vocational partnership with God. I am suggesting a view of the congregation as an ecology of care and an ecology of vocation. In this chapter we must explore further the nature of vocation, understood in relation to the Christian story and vision. And we must explore further too the character of the church as that covenant community that has a story powerful enough to bond people in the corporate and personal effort to find purposes for their lives which are part of the purposes of God. Walter Brueggemann has pointed to pastoral care as the enterprise of "nurturing folk into new metaphors."[1] As a theological foundation for this effort toward a practical theology of pastoral care undertaken in dialogue with faith-development theory, I want to explore the freshness and power of vocation and covenant as our fundamental metaphors.

VOCATION AND COMMUNITY

What do we mean by this term "vocation"? Of course we know that it comes from the Latin *vocare*, "to call," and *vocatio*, "call" or "calling." We know, further, that it is a word with particular relation to biblical religion. Traditionally it has referred to God's calling of particular persons or groups into a special relation with God. God's call to Abraham brought him into a covenant relation that eventually formed a partnership people. God's call to Moses led to the liberation of Israel from slavery and to the joining of a new covenant, under Torah, at Sinai. We remember Isaiah, Jeremiah, Amos, and those figures we call the lesser prophets, as persons with a calling. Nehemiah in exile, the Hebrew cupbearer to the Babylonian king, felt a calling to return to Jerusalem, the broken and corrupted capital, to lead in the rebuilding of its walls and the purification of its people. And in their own ways, Sarah, Judith, Naomi, Ruth, and even Rahab were called and in their faithfulness gave over their lives to furthering the purposes of God.

In the New Testament the term for calling is the Greek word *klesis* which means a "calling, invitation, summons" (usually *of* God, and *to* the religious life). It is related to the verb form *kaleo*, "I call, summon, or invite." The linkage with community is made explicit in the word *ekklesia*, which means literally a "calling out" and is used to refer to an "assembly, meeting, community, congregation, church, or society." In the New Testament, then, *klesis*, "calling, summons," refers to the special relationship to which all who became followers of Christ were called—a relationship of fidelity to God and of reliance upon God's promises. The *ekklesia* is the fellowship of those who have been called out by God into reconciled relation with one another and with God through Christ.

In the classic article "The History of the Word Vocation"[?] the Lutheran church historian Karl Holl traces the evolution of the Christian understanding of callings from New Testament times to modernity. Holl suggests that there is only one place in the New Testament where it is possible that *klesis* refers to one's occupation or to one's place of worldly work in the modern sense. We find this passage in 1 Cor. 7:20, where Saint Paul writes, "Each shall remain in the *klesis* to which he [she] was called." We cannot know for sure whether this use of *klesis* referred to occupation or position in the modern sense or whether it referred to a call to fidelity to the general call of all Christians in their relationship with God in Christ. Given the expectation of the imminent eschatological return of Christ in the earliest Christian community, it seems unlikely that Paul is making the case that one's station or place of worldly work has particular religious significance.

What is more certain, according to Holl, is that after the Christian faith became the religion of the Roman Empire, for many centuries callings were limited primarily to the priesthood and the monastic life. Ordinary Christians could of course be saved, but only bishops, priests, and monks had callings. We find the only exception to this in the early centuries of Christianity, when the dignity and sanction of a divine calling could be claimed for the emperor. Especially in the Byzantine Christian tradition it was believed that God appointed the ruler over God's people, thus giving rise to the powerful Christian version of the idea of the divine rights of kings.

Only in the late Middle Ages do we begin to see the first real linking of secular occupations and statuses to the concept of callings, a move in which worldly work gains some hint of religious significance. Curiously the first tenuous steps in the direction of giving daily secular work religious worth can be traced to the influences of the Neoplatonic imagery of the "great chain of being." Mediated by gnostic influences and by the writings of Plotinus and then, later, Dionysius the Areopagite, the late Middle Ages inherited the picturesque imagery of hierarchical ranks of terrestrial and celestial beings. This vision depicted the linkages connecting the forms of being, from the lowest forms of earthly life through, in ascending order, the higher animals, humanity, and the angelic heavenly hosts, to the very throne of God. In this conception every person as well as every being above and below humanity in the hierarchy had a definite place and rank. Deriving from this imagery, late Scholasticism projected an overall plan for Christian social life within which it sought to relate to each other the callings of religious folk and the callings of those who do secular work. This scheme, says Holl, is found broadly developed for the first time in the writings of Berthold of Regensburg.

Taking his start from Dionysius, who identified a hierarchy of nine angelic choirs, Berthold sees the human social order as divided into nine choirs. At the top stand three ruling choirs. In the first rank stands the pope; in the second are the spiritual people, that is, the bishops, priests, monks, and religious. In the third rank we find the secular magistrates, lords, and knights. Beneath these come the six lower choirs—from the garment makers "down to those who deal with medicine."⁴ Included in the list are all those who perform useful work and also the merchants. (Holl points out that Berthold must have had a particularly warm spot in his heart for the merchants, for whom he frequently puts in a good word.) Excluded from Berthold's list are all those who could not do their work and do right: usurers, hucksters, junk dealers, fiddlers and drummers, prostitutes, and armorers. His list also excluded those especially hated by Berthold, the penny (indulgence) preachers (who sound roughly equivalent to many of today's imperial TV preachers). All these people together made up the "tenth choir," that of the apostates who are directed by the devil.

In this scheme, the lower six choirs have religious significance, right of existence, and worth. But their worth is indirect and derived. Corresponding to the hierarchical view of Dionysius, their worth derives only from the fact that they serve the higher ranks and create for them what is necessary for life. The class and rank to which one belongs, in this scheme, is seen as a destiny placed upon one by God, to which, whether one likes it or not, one has to submit. Although this vision makes a place for a derived and secondary sort of religious significance for worldly work, it still excludes the possibility of an inner calling and direct religious connection for the lower classes and ranks.

Not until the thought of the fourteenth-century German mystics did there emerge an understanding of *all* human work as having the dignity, potentially, of a call. In this regard Holl points to the work of Meister Eckhart and his younger student and colleague Johann Tauler. According to Meister Eckhart's interpretation of 1 Cor. 7:20, "Not every one is called to God in the same way. . . . But even the lowest work and the lowest occupation is compatible with the demand of the highest. One can gather nettles," he adds, "and still stand in union with God." Johann Tauler relates as corroborating proof of this claim that a farmer was taken by surprise with an ecstasy while he was threshing. For that reason, Tauler thought, one can—and one should—remain in the class one was placed in by God. For Tauler the position in which one is placed is a "summons," a "call," that comes to one just as much as that inner call which was supposedly possessed by the monks and women religious. If one obeys this call with singleness of purpose, Tauler taught, one is truly on the way that leads to God.

Martin Luther brought to a kind of completion the extension to secular work of the dignity of a calling. His doctrine of justification by grace through faith removed the question of earning or meriting one's salvation through works or through work of any kind. Because we are justified by God's grace alone, any work, any office, if offered to God in faithfulness and gratitude, can be a fitting form of partnership with God in behalf of the neighbor. How do we serve God and love the neighbor? Luther answered, *In commune, per vocatione* (In community, through one's calling).

TOWARD A CONTEMPORARY UNDERSTANDING OF VOCATION

So far as I can tell, current usage of "vocation" as synonymous with "job, occupation, or career" dates from the latter part of the nineteenth century. This usage came with the emergence of increased technical specialization in post–Civil War industrial development and with the development of "vocational training" in the comprehensive high schools that the progressive era in education generated. Vocational education was the educational track one took if one intended to pursue neither a liberal arts course in higher education nor professional training as an engineer, physician, or lawyer. It implied the acquisition of job or occupational skills and certification. Because the concept of a vocation has been taken over by guidance counselors to refer to one's means of livelihood, there is a real question whether it can be reclaimed in its deeper, more inclusive, and radical sense. Yet there is something at stake here that we cannot afford to give up on too quickly. The mystics of the fourteenth century based their recognition that secular statuses and work have a worth equal to the status and work of the religious classes on the recognition that God's spirit and presence sometimes illumined the hearts of peasants and farmers and shoemakers as fully and radiantly as those of monks, nuns, and priests.

There is a clue of tremendous importance here. Secular callings or work can be places of service to, and a deep relation with, God. To be "in vocation" one need not be involved in the work of constant prayer or sacrificial deprivation of the self. And more, in the tradition of *vocatio* there is the conviction that our place, our office, our vocation, is not merely a destiny to which God assigns us but a place of creative partnership to which God calls us and in which God chooses to meet us and bring our work to some significant contribution to the purposes of God.

Novelist, preacher, and essayist, Frederick Buechner writes,

> [Vocation] comes from the Latin *vocare*, to call, and means the work one is called to by God.
>
> There are all different kinds of voices calling you to do all different kinds of work, and the problem is to find out which is the voice of God rather than of Society, say, or the Superego, or Self-Interest.
>
> By and large a good rule for finding out is this. The kind of work God usually calls you to is the kind of work (a) that you need most to do and (b) that the world most needs to have done. If you really get a kick out of your work, you've presumably met requirement (a), but if your work is writing deodorant commercials, the chances are you've missed requirement (b). On the other hand, if your work is being a doctor in a leper colony, you have probably met requirement (b), but if most of the time you are bored and depressed by it, the chances are you have not only bypassed (a) but probably aren't helping your patients much either.
>
> Neither the hair shirt nor the soft berth will do. *The place God calls you to is the place where your deep gladness and the world's deep hunger meet.*[5]

I want to build on this legacy from the fourteenth century mystics and from Luther. But I want to go beyond them and, to some degree, beyond Buechner too. For Buechner, all the beauty of what he says notwithstanding, tends to limit one's vocation to one's work or job.

Vocation cannot be reduced to our work or our occupation. Vocation is bigger than our careers or our professions, though it may include both. Vocation is the response we make with our *total selves* to the call of God (acknowledged or unacknowledged) and to God's call to partnership. In this more comprehensive sense, vocation refers to the orchestration of our leisure, our relationships, our work, our private lives, our public lives, and the resources we steward. It is the focusing of our lives in the service of God and in the love of the neighbor.[6]

If this language about partnership with God seems too glib, let us try to translate it. Vocation, we might say, is the pattern of our lives' energies and involvements as directed in the service of our strongest love or devotion. Vocation is the pattern of our work, our relations, our leisure, and our private and public lives which results from the dominant intention, passion, or drive of our lives. Vocation is linked to and grounded in that place in our heart where we recognize that we are intended for some purpose beyond mere survival. It grows out of the intuition that we are called for some purpose beyond self-aggrandizement or the self-interested pursuit of pleasure. It grows out of the intuition that we are intended to be about more than mere self-actualization. Vocation derives from that profound sense that we are called into existence in this time and this place and among these people for the sake of investing our gifts and potentials in furthering some cause that is of transcending importance.

VOCATION AND COVENANT COMMUNITY

The understanding of community which goes with vocation is that of covenant. Here again we deal with a big word that has biblical roots. And here again we encounter a strong word that is often corrupted in contemporary usage. Not long ago a very frank television producer jarred a church historian who served as consultant for a program on the idea of covenant in American democracy. The producer said, "You recognize, don't you, that for most of your listeners 'covenant' will mean an agreement signed among the residents of posh neighborhoods that they will keep certain racial or ethnic groups out."

Covenant represents both an idea and a root metaphor for community.

A root metaphor for community is an image drawn from a universal dimension of human experience that provides the generative basis for the extrapolation of a comprehensive normative representation of human life in a polity or society. Covenant as a root metaphor derives from the universal human experience of promise making and promise keeping as the basis for solidarity and lasting relations in community. In the biblical legacy that informs the life of the church, covenant community is brought into being by the call and promises of God.[7]

We may better understand covenant as a root metaphor for community if we contrast it with two other common and powerful root metaphors for community—those of organism and contract. In the organismic metaphor the basic experience and image is that of a body—a biological organism. As in the experience of organic growth, there is a kind of natural unfolding of growth or change in the community as body. A second reference for the organic model is the extended family, usually with patriarchal authority. Like organs and limbs, members of organic communities have their specific places and functions. They are not interchangeable; their management is not subject to rational bureaucratic planning and decision making. Governance is usually exercised by an elite that is assumed to be fitted by birth and natural endowment, by ascribed status, or by divine sanction in religious communities, to exercise that function. Tradition, as interpreted by the leadership elite, is usually the strongest normative reference and source of justification for decision and action in the community. Often communities encourage belief in the sinfulness and inadequacy in self-governing ability of the masses or majority, thus strengthening reliance upon the leadership elite.

The pre-Vatican II Roman Catholic church had strong elements of the organic model. Many local congregations of Protestant churches, particularly rural ones, provide miniature instances of organic communities. The Greek Orthodox communion appears to preserve a strongly organic character. Elements of a "mystery-mastery" approach to authority[8] flourish in such communions. Change, when it comes, must be made to appear as an evolutionary development, sanctioned through its extension of tradition, and not altering in fundamental ways the organic structure of the community.

The root metaphor of social contract derives from a secularization of the idea of covenant. It had its modern rise in the seventeenth-century development of classical political and economic theory in Hobbes, Locke, and later, Adam Smith. These thinkers were faced with the problem of grounding the legitimacy of state authority after the breakdown of ecclesial legitimation in the Reformation and the subsequent wars of religion, and after the decline of the doctrine of the divine right of kings. Their solution was to locate rights and authority in the individual, understood as a self-interested but rational agent. Civil authority can be constituted, they taught, if each individual is thought of as relinquishing some part of his freedom and authority and investing the central authority with it. In this way the sovereign or central civil authority derives the right, power, and responsibility to govern as a kind of impartial umpire. Members of the contractual community may pursue their individual notions of the good, but only insofar as they do not interfere with the rights of their co-contractarians to the similar exercise of their freedom. In this conception, membership in the polity contributes nothing to the formation of the moral self. The individual is presumed to be morally formed by agents other than law or the state, and to have formed interests that are beyond the concern of the state. Only when impinging upon their neighbors' like pursuit of individual notions of the good do the goals and purposes of members become the concern of civil authority.

In the contractarian root metaphor, community is understood as the product of the will and volition of autonomous moral individuals. Community is the creature of their having formed a compact or contract: it can be modified or rescinded if it no longer meets or serves the ends of a majority of the members. Among religious traditions, certain forms of congregationalism are subject to contractarian interpretation. Practically speaking, the administrative boards, ruling elders, vestries, deacons, and other official governing groups of congregations in *all* polities in this country often understand their responsibilities in terms of the individualism of contractarian assumptions.

In contrast to the organic root metaphor, where community has its origins in the mythic past, and to the contractual metaphor, where community results from the utilitarian inventiveness of the individuals who make it up, covenant grounds a community called into being from beyond itself. Community membership comes neither as a fate nor a choice but as a being-chosen. Belonging is based neither on the ascriptive belonging of traditional communities nor on the self-interested initiative of contract. Rather, it comes by way of gradual assent and conformation with a community of called ones.

Covenant and vocation go together. In a covenant community persons with different callings are bound together with common loyalties to a cause" or to beliefs and values that are bigger than they. It does not particularly matter whether the persons like one another or not. It is not important whether they would have chosen to be yoked together or tied up with these particular others or not. In a covenant community, for the sake of shared loyalty to the cause for which the community came into being, they work at relations of mutual trust and loyalty with their companions in community, and with the cause that animates its purpose.

Covenant community recognizes the social character of the self. It celebrates our interdependence with one another. It recognizes that we join institutions for mixtures of self-interest and loyalty to the causes for which the institutions exist. Its disciplines aim toward the development of capacities for responsibility to and partnership with the action of God. It aims to awaken, call forth, support, and keep accountable the vocations of each of its members for partnership with God, and for covenant existence with one another. It is called—and aims to be—an ecology of vocations.

Leadership in a covenant community is not hierarchical. There are different gifts and different functions, but each vocation claims equality with all others in relation to the One who initiates the covenant. There is equality in the worth of the vocational contributions of all the members (1 Corinthians 12; Romans 12).

The church as covenant community derives its purposes from the will and intent of the One who initiates the covenant and calls us into covenant relation. It exists for partnership in God's creative work, God's work of judgment and governance, and God's work of redemption and liberation. Our membership derives from specific covenants having their roots in the particular events and relations of our lives. Some of these were made on our behalf before we could choose; others derive from our response to having been chosen, when we reach a more responsible age. Either way, our assent one to another in covenant community is not initially voluntary. We come to a more conscious assent and we come to take on joyful intentionality in covenant-belonging as we grow and mature in faith.

CHAPTER 3

God's Work
and
Our Vocations

Practical theology, as we have viewed it, is critical and constructive reflection "arising out of and giving guidance to a community of faith in the *praxis* of its mission [and] leading to ongoing modification and development of the ways the church shapes its life to be in partnership with God's work in the world." That definition and the discussion of vocation in Chapter 2 focus for us an unavoidable set of questions. If vocation is "finding a purpose for our lives that is part of the purposes of God" and if vocation is the "response we make with our total selves to the call of God to partnership," then how shall we discern and speak of God's action and our response? If the community of faith is to align itself in vocational partnership with the intention and working of God, how are we to understand and interpret the divine *praxis*? The responses we make to these questions are determinative for a practical theology of pastoral care.

GOD'S WORK: THREE CLASSICAL METAPHORS

Theology does its reflective and constructive work by way of metaphor. The etymology of the word "metaphor" is helpful: the Greek *meta*, "across, over, beyond," and *pherein*, "to bear or carry." Metaphor, we may say, is the use of an evocative representation of something from our common experience to "carry us over" toward experiential participation in something otherwise not accessible to our experiencing. When we speak of God metaphorically we may say, "The Lord is my shepherd." Or we may say with the prophet, "Our God is a refiner's fire."

When we examine the Bible's use of metaphors in the representation of God, we note three special features. First, the Bible uses multiple metaphors for evoking awareness of the character and action of God. This is to avoid reductionism and idolatry. Deeply suspicious of substituting carved images for the reality of the living God, ancient Israel carefully guarded the sanctity of the divine name. To avoid reification the Israelites referred to the holy One in a multiplicity of metaphorical representations that depict the actions and attitudes of God. Second, biblical metaphors are relational metaphors. The Bible knows nothing of God in terms of some divine essence apart from God's self-disclosure in creation and to human-kind in redemption. The biblical God is not some prime mover or some abstract and metaphysical principle. Rather, God is as God has been made manifest in relational initiatives of grace and judgment, of covenant initiation and steadfast faithfulness. And third, in relation to the principal metaphors for God in the biblical tradition, there are other metaphors depicting and evoking awareness of the shape of human responsiveness and partnership with God. Each of the principal metaphoric representa-tions of God implies or calls forth a correlative form of human relation and participation.

Across his thirty years of teaching at the Yale Divinity School, H. Richard Niebuhr identified three principal biblically derived metaphors for divine activity and human response. He spoke of God's work as crea-tor, as governor, and as liberator-redeemer. Niebuhr constructed his inter-pretation of these metaphors—and of the correlative metaphors for human response and partnership that go with them—along lines that moved well beyond the anthropomorphism and anthropocentrism of clas-sical theism. I find an approach such as his indispensable for a practical theology of pastoral care oriented toward helping persons discern and respond to the activity of God.[1]

In what follows I will build on the analysis Niebuhr developed in his lecture course on ethics. Niebuhr must not be held responsible, however, for what I have hung from the scaffolding of his thought. Nor should Jürgen Moltmann[2] and Langdon Gilkey[3] be blamed for what I have taken from them by way of inspiration and insight in the development of this chapter.

THE CREATIVE WORK OF GOD

When we try to bring to mind our images of God's work as creator what do we find? Let me suggest this exercise: spend a moment reflecting, remembering, imagining God's work as creator. Try to be in touch with the rootage of your imagery of God's creative action.

When I follow my own admonition I find my memory and emotions drawn to the depiction in language and music of the account of creation given in James Weldon Johnson's *God's Trombones*.⁴ I was in my early teens when I first encountered this imagery, inspired in Johnson by the traditions of black preaching. I remember it vividly, though I have not returned to the text for something over thirty years:

> And God stepped out on space,
> And he looked around and said:
> I'm lonely—
> I'll make me a world.
>
> And far as the eye of God could see
> Darkness covered everything,
> Blacker than a hundred midnights
> Down in a cypress swamp.
>
> Then God smiled,
> And the light broke,
> And the darkness rolled up on one side,
> And the light stood shining on the other,
> And God said: That's good!
>
> Then God reached out and took the light in his hands,
> And God rolled the light around in his hands
> Until he made the sun;
> And he set that sun a-blazing in the heavens.
> And the light that was left from making the sun
> God gathered it up in a shining ball
> And flung it against the darkness,
> Spangling the night with the moon and stars.
> Then down between
> The darkness and the light
> He hurled the world;
> And God said: That's good!

Admittedly, my teenage ears and eyes were not jarred, as they would be now, by Johnson's use of all the male pronouns. If we continue the quotation, however, to the point where he talks about the creation of humankind, we will find the following lines, where all the masculine imagery for God receives a decisive maternal qualification:

> And there the great God Almighty
> Who lit the sun and fixed it in the sky,
> Who flung the stars to the most far corner of the night,
> Who rounded the earth in the middle of his hand;

> This Great God,
> Like a mammy bending over her baby,
> Kneeled down in the dust
> Toiling over a lump of clay
> Till he shaped it in his own image.

Jürgen Moltmann in his 1984 Gifford Lectures' gives us a very different picture, almost at the other extreme from Johnson's anthropomorphic imagery. Grounded in Trinitarian doctrine, Moltmann invites us to contemplate the dynamic eternal community within God's self—the creative power, the Logos of divine wisdom, and the energizing spirit—interacting in dynamic, full, and complete unity, and internal richness. Creation begins, in Moltmann's reinterpretation of the Christian classic, not with a handful of primal substance but with the divine being making space for other being within God's Trinitarian life. Noting the love and humility of God which make the space for being other than God to appear, Moltmann too appeals to maternal images. Implicitly, he invites us to imagine this space as the womb of creation. Then by God's word, from and within this space there is world. Christian tradition affirms that God created the world *ex nihilo*—out of and from nothing. *Deus dixit*, God speaks, and the universe, in vastly contracted form, is born. In this vision there is not some primeval substance or chaos upon which God imposed order. Rather, order, or the seeds of order, came with the creation of matter, space, and time, out of nothingness.

Strangely, this biblical account, elaborated in Christian tradition, corresponds in thoroughly compatible ways with the now-dominant theory held by theoretical physicists regarding the origins of the universe—the so-called big bang theory. As British physicist Paul Davies has written, this theory "proposes that the entire cosmos came into existence in a huge explosion." Davies continues,

> The nature of the big bang is frequently misconceived for it is often presented as the explosion of a lump of material in a pre-existing void. But . . . there *is* no space outside the universe. Rather, it is more accurate to envisage the big bang as an event in which space itself came into being. In fact, the scientific picture of the creation is, in this respect, more profound than the biblical, for it represents the origin not only of matter, but of space too. Space came out of the big bang, and not the other way round. The big bang, then was not an event which occurred within the universe; it was the coming-into-being of the universe, in its entirety, from literally nothing.[6]

Not only space and matter came into being with creation, but time as well. Approximately fifteen billion years of time have made it possible for the highly concentrated, explosive beginning to expand into what Davies describes as a "universe full of clusters of galaxies, thousands and thousands of millions of them, distributed evenly throughout space. Galaxies are the building blocks of the cosmos."[7]

We have to stretch our minds to their limit to try to conceive the macrocosmic vastness of this expanding universe. Even now, astrophysicists tell us, there are galactic regions where stars and planets are being formed under immense pressures and at stupendous temperatures. In a way resonant with Moltmann's use of motherly images for the initial creation, the scientists call these regions the "maternity ward of the universe."

To a layman it is fascinating to see theoretical physicists beginning again to celebrate the lawfulness, order, symmetry, and beauty of the expanding universe. Apparently, since Maxwell's brilliant reconciling of the theories of magnetic and electrical forces in the mid-nineteenth century, and Einstein's theory of space-time relativity in the early twentieth, and the discovery in the last twenty years of the forces that, in balance, maintain the structure of the atom, scientists have begun to conceive of a unified field theory that promises to account for the patterns and dynamics characterizing the behavior of matter, from the most infinitesimal microcosmic particles to the greatest of the galaxies. When the theoretical physicists begin to speak of a superforce—the combined and integrated effects of the four basic forces that maintain pattern and symmetry in the universe—it should not be surprising that a theologian thinks of the loving energy and unifying spirit of a creative God.

And then the Christian classic says that God created humankind—male and female—in God's own image. In a pattern suggesting extraordinary planfulness, we see an expanding universe that exhibits growing complexity while maintaining an ever-growing internal richness. Theologians and physicists alike call us to see that all matter and all being exist in relational nets and in a vast interdependence. Using the old term "nature" to include both living and inanimate entities in creation, humans are reminded that we are part of nature. Moltmann, in one of the most creative dimensions of his new theology of creation, suggests that humankind, deeply rooted in membership in nature, has the special calling to be the *reflective* part of creation. It is creation as a whole that is to be the image of God, Moltmann insists. Humankind is that part of nature in which its awareness of relatedness and kinship with God has formed. Humankind is called to increasing degrees of conscious partnership with God in the ongoing elaboration and perfection of creation toward God's ends. This does not separate us from nature, however. Rather, it gives us a growing awareness of our kinship with, membership in, and custodial responsibility for brother earth and sister nature. And more, it means that the creativity of nature—which is part of its mirroring of the image of God—is peculiarly and precariously concentrated in the human sphere of nature. God seems willing to take the risk of a special kind of growing partnership with our kind. In a way that seems to put earth and nature at risk, God welcomes human creatures to a qualitatively new kind of participation in God's ongoing work of creation.

GOD'S WORK OF GOVERNANCE

Our effort to elaborate the outline of a theology of God's creative work led us to see that there is a purposefulness and an intentional structure built into the space, time, and matter that came into being in creation. The new universe is filled with purposeful potential. From the beginning, the forces that maintain symmetry and order in the expanding universe are present and active. They create rhythms, patterns, and planfulness in the universe. And yet God includes in creation the open texture of new possibility. Though there is a lawfulness to the ways elements can be combined, there is no predetermination of the range of possible combinations. Although the building blocks of the universe are not infinitely malleable, there is in the texture of creation a great deal of flexibility. There is room for spontaneity, serendipity, and novelty.

When we reach the human level of nature we can speak of this open texture of creation in terms of freedom. And yet, in an analogous way, nature at every level exhibits something very like freedom.

Freedom, though real and consequential, is always limited by what may be called destiny.[a] This is true at every systems level in nature. Destiny, at any systems level, is constituted by all the givens that characterize an entity. At the human level, destiny includes our genetic makeup, the influence of our environment, the limits and possibilities of our native language, and the shaping power of the stories, symbols, and ideas we inherit. At the human level, destiny includes the consequences of past choices made by or for us. Destiny, in any present, is the result of previous resolutions of the tension between destiny and freedom. Perhaps the point begins to become clear: destiny at the human level is made up of all that impinges upon and within us as constraint and as support, as limit and as resource.

Freedom is given to us—in creation and in each moment—as the open texture of possibility that can modify destiny. Because God has intention for creation, in God's ongoing creativity we are given the gift of possibility and freedom in each new moment. It is a gift from God who is the power of the future. With freedom there comes, at the human level, the gift of imagination, the capacity to envision new possibilities, and the ability to choose—or to be chosen by—possibilities.

In the interplay of destiny and freedom, and in the face of God's gift of the possibility of freedom toward God's intended future, we see the powerful reality that the Christian classic calls sin. What is sin? In this perspective we can see sin as the tendency of creatures, acting in destiny and freedom, to veer away from God's intended future—a future of complementarity and mutuality within being, a future of the fulfillment of creation. Sin is the tendency to allow the dynamism of destiny and freedom, intended by God to lead us toward God's future, to be veered off into "fatedness." In fatedness, destinies and freedom become congealed in destructive forms that are in enmity against God's future. Fatedness represents side pockets of stagnation in creation. In fatedness there is a combining of inheritances of antinature destinies which subvert freedom and put it in bondage.

In the Christian classic there is a strong tradition that links the Logos—the Word of God, the wisdom of God, the eternal Christ of God—with creation. John's Gospel begins, "In the beginning was the Word [Logos] and the Word was with God and the Word was God. The Logos was in the beginning with God. All things came into being through the Logos; and apart from the Logos nothing came into being that has come into being." We need to see the roles of the Logos in creation against the backdrop of our talk about destiny, freedom, and fatedness. We may understand the Logos in creation as a structure that intends righteousness in the processes of history. The Logos is a structure of reason, wisdom, and lawfulness built into the very heart of things. It is designed to guide and lure the interplay of destiny and freedom toward God's intended future.

In many ways and in many centuries the world's great religious traditions have in their classics brought to expression efforts to formulate the imperatives of this structure that intends righteousness at the heart of the world processes. The tao, understood as *way;* torah understood as *law* or *way;* the "eightfold path" of Buddhism; dharma in Hinduism; the law of love as articulated by Jesus; the idea of natural law as taught in Stoicism—all these symbols represent efforts to formulate and make visible in different ways a structure that intends righteousness in the process of human life. They all represent approaches that try to keep freedom and destiny open to the ideal possibilities and future that come as divine gifts.

God's governing action, then, is this structure intending righteousness in the processes of history. It is an expression of God's love and grace. It seeks to form and orient men and women for the freedom and wholeness of God's intended future. It aims to prevent the cumulative souring of destiny and to guard against the veering of destiny and freedom into the destructive stagnation of fatedness.

Although the Logos, as the structure intending righteousness, is an expression of God's love and grace in creation, when we go against it we experience it as the destructiveness of a brutal judgment. As the theologian James Cone has put it, the other side of the love of God is the wrath of God. Of course, in order to be able to see this wrath of God we must take a longer perspective than the three- to five-year plans most of us are used to pursuing.

Martin Luther King, Jr., captures this understanding of God's governing activity when he says, "The arc of history bends slowly, but it bends towards justice." And Paul Tillich testifies to it when he says, "Humans in history do not so much break the laws of God as we break ourselves upon them."

Given sufficient time, corrupt and brutalizing regimes collapse as much from internal flaws and failures as from external resistance and counterforce. This is why societies and governments based on the economic foundations of slavery and exploitation are inherently unstable and carry within themselves the seeds of their own destruction.

Conscience is the subjective reference we have for the presence of a structure that intends righteousness in the processes of history. Martin Buber offers us both a testimony to the power of conscience and another witness to the foundations of a universal lawfulness. He says,

Existential guilt occurs when someone injures an order of the human world whose foundations he knows and recognizes as those of his own existence and of all common human existence.[9]

GOD'S WORK OF LIBERATION
AND REDEMPTION

In personal life and in the lives of nations and societies, fatedness at times becomes the reigning power. That is to say, sin becomes the dominant mode and structure of our lives. This is a potential at *any* time. At points it becomes a terrible personal and collective reality. The Christian doctrine of the Fall insists that were it not for God's continuing work of liberation and redemption, the bondage of humanity and nature to fatedness would become complete.

By God's work of liberation and redemption we mean all the ways God acts to offset the consequences of our misuse of freedom. Here we have in mind all the ways God seeks to reclaim, heal, restore, and reconcile humankind, mired in destructive fatedness, to God's intended fulfillment of creation in a commonwealth of love and justice.

In the Christian classic the paradigmatic acts of divine liberation and redemption begin with Noah's redemption from a fallen and corrupt world and his rejoining to God in the covenant of the rainbow sign. It continues with Abraham's summons from the bondage of false worship and into a covenant relation with Yahweh, who promised to make of Abraham and Sarah the parents of a covenant nation. The story goes on with God's redemption of Israel from slavery in Egypt and the institution of a covenant relation based upon torah—the way of holiness and righteousness. Continuing in prophet and liberator and in the periodic renewal of covenant, the biblical story culminates in the radical renewal and universalization of the covenant in the incarnation.

In Jesus the Christ the Christian classic sees the paramount expression of the liberating and redeeming love of God. The same love of God which gave rise to creation confirms itself as utterly faithful to the created through entering into the Godforsaken spaces in creation taken up by the moral sourness of corrupted destiny and freedom. "The Logos became a human being," as John 1:14 says. And to those who receive the Logos, he becomes the light and life that restores freedom, possibility, and covenant relatedness to God, to the neighbor, and to nature.

God's explicit entering into history in Jesus Christ means collision with the structures of fatedness. It means immersion in the congealed pools of subverted destiny and freedom. It means bringing the spirit of new creation powerfully into contact with the corrupted and resistive spirit of being in bondage to sin. By this explicit entering, God makes God manifest—God glorifies Godself—in the cleansing encounter with the human oppression and suffering that arise from our sinfulness.

In the cross of Christ, in a double manifestation—a double glorification—we see the bringing together of two overwhelming realities. On the one hand we see in the rending of the holy man, Jesus the Christ, the depth, destructiveness, and Godforsakenness of the fatedness that infests the structures of our common life. On the other hand, we see in the cross in fiercely consolidated and focused form, the radical extreme to which the divine power of God's liberating and redemptive love goes to bring us into new creation.

VOCATION AND PARTNERSHIP WITH GOD

In this extended discussion of three major metaphors derived from the biblical tradition, we have tried to say something about what God is doing in creation, in governance, and in liberation and redemption. Our interest is practical in trying to find symbols and formulations that can help us see and discern God's purposes and ways of acting. Biblical metaphors for God, we pointed out earlier, are always correlative. They never focus just upon God and God's action, but they depict God's action as related to creation, and as correlated to human action. Our practical interest lies in clarifying our callings as human beings—our vocations as those who are called to be in partnership with God in God's work of creation, governance, and liberation and redemption.

PARTNERSHIP WITH GOD'S WORK OF ONGOING CREATION

Partnership with God's work of ongoing creation indeed means many things. Foundationally it means participation in the procreative and nurturing processes. Whether by biological parenting, or by the investment of care in the children and youth of our common trust, it means being part of the treasuring of each child as a gift of God. It means contributing to the nurture of persons toward wholeness and richness of contribution to the common good. This involves us in education—religious and secular. It means trying to form persons who can take their place as interdependent citizens of a commonwealth of love and justice that is inclusive of other people but that is also inclusive of the larger community of nature of which we are but a part.

This leads to a second set of considerations. To be part of God's creative work means to be intentionally involved in the maintenance and extension of an ecology of care—an ecology of care for persons and for the environment. Care for the environment means, of course, care for the earth, our shared household; and for nature, our mother. It also includes care for the environment of spirit—for culture. Our calling to partnership in God's work of creation should include the conscious construction of images in architecture, city planning, and conservation. It includes the generation of images in the arts, literature, drama, music, and religion.

A central part of our calling to work in God's creative action comes in the cultivation and extension of the capacities of the earth to support multiplying life. This means the furthering of ecologically just agriculture. It means the development of equitable and honest systems of food distribution. It means the cleansing and restoration of waters. And it means the elaboration—and keeping under humane constraint—of that most creative and productive engine of the twentieth century, the modern corporation.

To be part of the creative work of God must increasingly mean in the areas of science and technology a rejoining of science and spirituality. It requires—dare I say it?—that science come to understand itself in some significant ways as *theology*. What do I mean by this? In part, it is to suggest that science as it probes the further mysteries of the universe for understanding is involved profoundly in tracing the thoughts of God. Or better, it means following the remarkable interplay of destiny and freedom, at every systems level, seeking to discern the ideal possibilities God intended—and nature produced—to constitute the intricate balances that maintain the beauty and symmetry of the universe. Such a reflective and reverent science can help us in the great ethical tasks that come not only with being imitators of what God has created but with being imitators of and participants in the very divine creativity itself. We must develop a spiritual and ethically discerning science to enable us to ask when the technological elaboration and employment of scientific possibilities runs in accordance with the trajectory of divine creativity, and when it does not. Only a science combining ethical and spiritual sensitivities with bold investigative brilliance can help us keep an evolving earth moving in the direction of being the image of its creator.

PARTNERSHIP WITH GOD'S GOVERNANCE

The perspective on God's creation we have developed here reminds us that through the Logos—the reason, the order, the wisdom of God—there is in creation a structuring that intends righteousness in the processes of history. Further, we are reminded that human beings, like nature at every level, live in the contingent tension of destiny and freedom. Freedom is the gift of ideal possibility which God's grace gives us from the future fulfillment of creation which God intends. Freedom gives corporate and personal destiny to some degree an open texture. Sin is that tendency, present in all human beings and perhaps in other dimensions of nature, to be drawn away from the frightening openness of the future and from the tensions between freedom and destiny, and into fatedness. Put more strongly, sin is the tendency to preempt the open texture of freedom God provides us, in the midst of our corporate and personal destinies, and to turn it toward the assertion of our own defensive and self-aggrandizing passions. Sin, in this sense, becomes a structural warp of our communities and institutions; it becomes an ethos of exploitation and greed, of numbness and victimization.

Partnership in the governing action of God means, therefore, attempting to discern and find public language for the plumb lines that can help us see our personal and institutional lives in relation to the structures that intend righteousness in God's governance. Surely this means a call to corporate moral seriousness about learning and teaching not just the formulations of lawfulness in torah, tao, dharma, and the gospel but the spirit and deep principles of that lawfulness. Surely it means holding up a discipline of life in our communities of faith in which we try to form ourselves—and those whom we nurture as parents, teachers, religious leaders, managers and officers, legislators and politicians—in accordance with that justice which is immanent in God's governing activity.

Moreover, to take sin seriously means to recognize the realism of vigilance, coupled with skillful and determined discernment of exploitation and abuses of the common good. Though corrupt regimes carry within themselves the seeds of their own destruction, they can on the way to their demise inflict vast and vicious damage upon the innocent. Though commercial greed and environmentally destructive business practices generally bring about their own correction, they can inflict irreversible damage on the earth and on present and future generations before they collide with the divine lawfulness. Partnership with the divine governing action therefore includes the realism of active restraint of wrongdoing—beginning with parental restraint. It includes the necessary and legitimate restraint imposed by law and enforced by the majesty and force of justly established governments. Part of the destiny of democratic governments is the gift—by no means easy to create—of institutions that have been established and maintained to promote the interests of the common good and to preserve the human and civil rights of their citizens. God's governing action requires an active, persistent, courageous, and resourceful public involvement in keeping the destiny of democracy responsive to God's gift of freedom toward God's commonwealth of love and justice. Governments and political economies are perpetually and permeably threatened through both the banal forms of evil deriving from the greed and shortsightedness of their citizens and the more corporate and conspiratorial ruthlessness of organized despoilers. Faithfulness in partnership with God's governing action means developing the character, the means, and the will to enforce decency and to maintain good order through just law. Cooperation with God's work of governance, under the criteria of God's intended commonwealth of love and justice, means endeavoring to make punishment—individual and corporate—restorative rather than merely punitive. It means endeavoring to keep the common resources of the people in the service of the common good. It means resistance to oppression and commitment to the effort to avoid violent revolutions by changing revolting conditions.

Persons engaged in partnership with the governing action of God believe, hope, act, and repent in the conviction that God is involved as the structure intending righteousness in the complex struggles of contending nations and parties. They believe that determined and effective opposition to private exploitation and organized intimidation will call forth resourceful support. They maintain hope and integrity in the conviction that persons who live—and if necessary, die—in the preserving or the bringing about of justice are not acting alone but are in alignment with the very grain of the universe, and that their cause will be vindicated.

PARTNERSHIP IN THE
LIBERATIVE AND REDEMPTIVE
WORK OF GOD

There is a real sense in which we can be—and often are—involved in God's work of creation and even of governance without being particularly conscious or intentional about it. It is part of the working of what traditionally we have called God's providence that many of us—and all of us at times in our lives—have been employed in the work of God despite our own motives or our intentions to be about the pursuit of our own interests. By virtue of being parents, for example, we are, without necessarily intending it, part of God's creative work. By work or self-investment that rewards us, we may also be contributing to medical health, to aesthetic enjoyment, to the production of goods and services, or to a corporation's development. Similarly, many political leaders, through doing what will make them electable or reelectable to higher office, advocate policies and provide leadership that may well turn out to have been part of the governing work of God. The providence of God and the reasonably healthy social and political arrangements of a society may assure that merely through the pursuit of our own interest and self-fulfillment we necessarily involve ourselves in a certain amount of cooperation in God's work.

The closer we get to God's work of liberation and redemption, however, the less likely it is that the pursuit of self-interest or of conventional notions of duty will insure our being in partnership with God. In the reasonably just arrangements of good societies there are still many persons trapped in the conditions of bondage—bondage of the spirit, leading to greed, misuse of power, and exploitation; bondage of the will, leading to addiction, mental anguish, and abuse of others; and bondage to evil imaginations of the heart, leading to corruption and destructiveness. And worse, there are vast and powerful institutions the very structures of which are premised on death-dealing offensiveness and defensiveness.

Moreover, there are many societies and nations where the polity and political economy have become the vehicles for the aggrandizement of elites at the price of dehumanizing the people and despoiling common resources. In such contexts, political, social, and economic liberation are inseparably tied to God's work of liberation and redemption.

We do well to remember that in the Christian classic, the central paradigm for human cooperation in the liberative and redemptive work of God is to be found in the incarnation—God's becoming human and submitting to death on the cross. At the heart of the Christian understanding of incarnation is the reality of *kenosis*—literally, the self-emptying, the pouring out of the very self of God.

In any Christian understanding of the human vocation to partnership with God, all self- or class-aggrandizing images are undercut by the paradigm of the incarnation. Partnership in the divine creativity and the divine governance are to be understood, Christianly, through the lenses of God emptying self in radical love, to reclaim, restore, and rehabilitate persons and societies.

Here we come up against the mystery and the sometimes terrible cost of vocation. For here the focus is on Christ, whom we must follow to the foot of the cross. From the foot of the cross we see the mystery of God's love poured out for us and for *all* sinners. Here we see the mystery of a vast reconciliation bought at the price of God's suffering—the pain of God.

To be part of the liberative and redemptive work of God means entering into solidarity with Christ and his suffering. It therefore means solidarity with those among whom he said he would be found, the "little ones"—the oppressed, the sick, the poor, the prisoner, the widow, the orphan, the addict, the leper, the AIDS victim, the "missing ones." But it also means being among those with whom Jesus placed himself—the alienated sinners represented by the zealots and the public women, and the confident sinners symbolized by the tax franchisers. And we must recognize and repent of our solidarity with the betraying and abandoning disciples and of our kinship with the compromised and compromising officials of temple and empire.

If our solidarity with Christ is genuine, we too will not be exempt from the pain of God. We too will find, with Simone Weil,[10] that being at the foot of the cross, which is situated in the midst of Godforsakenness, is a place of intimate fellowship and communion with God.

The point is this: As we become more intentional about embracing God's call to partnership, as we grow in the capacity to be part of the reflective image of God, we stand increasingly under the imperative to submit *our* equations of destiny-freedom and fatedness to God's liberative and redemptive work. Without liberation from our obsessions with survival, security, and significance, we will not have the resources of spirit to be part of the liberation of others. Without liberation from our Egypts of the mind and of the heart, we will not have the moral strength to be agents of justice. Without redemption from the fear of freedom that comes with God's gift of possibility toward God's future, and without liberation from the torpor of our fatedness, we will subtly use our human strength to defend ourselves and to bless the present order.

As surgeons must be highly trained if they will heal rather than harm, those of us who intend to grow in being partners in God's liberative and redemptive work must undergo the cleansing and liberating cauterizing of heart and soul that will fit us to be instruments of God's new creation.

CHAPTER 4

Stages in Selfhood
and Faith

The previous chapter's effort to provide a perspective on the modes of divine action—the divine *praxis*—and of human response in partnership, inevitably has a kind of Himalayan quality. With that sort of overview we can see the towering peaks, but only at a distance. That there is value in such a perspective is, I hope, obvious. Within the present chapter, however, I want to use a telescopic lens that will enable us to move in much closer. The objective will be to recognize some of the patterns of struggle, growth, and change that characterize human beings in the process of becoming aware, conscious, and increasingly responsive and responsible selves, as partners with God.

How do we human beings, as that species in nature who have the special calling to a *reflective* partnership with God, develop toward the fulfillment of this calling? Is there a conceptual paradigm that can illumine the paths by which we emerge toward an accountable awareness of ourselves, others, and our action worlds as responsive to God's action?

For more than a dozen years I have been working at the intersection of theology and developmental psychology in the effort to shape such a perspective on faith and selfhood. In the constructive-developmental theories of Jean Piaget,[1] Lawrence Kohlberg,[2] Robert Selman,[3] and others, I have found helpful resources with which a practical theology can engage in the effort to account for how we become subjects before and in relation to God. In this chapter I want to offer a fresh account of the stage theory of faith development on which I have written at length in other places.[4] This discussion of the stages, however, will be enriched in two ways that are important for our present concerns. First, I will bring the consideration of stages of faith more explicitly into the theological framework offered in the last chapter than has previously been possible. To see faith development theory as a contribution to theological anthropology has been an intent of mine all along. The present writing, in its accentuation of theological foundations of pastoral care, provides a good context to pursue that intent. Second, I will develop here a correlation of stages of faith with stages of selfhood, particularly as focused in the work of Robert Kegan.[5] Kegan has made a central contribution to the constructivist developmental family of theories by extending the Piaget and Kohlberg paradigms in the direction of ego development and personality theory. Through dialogue with his work, and by drawing upon an important interpretation of our two perspectives given by Steven S. Ivy,[6] it will be possible, I believe, to communicate in new ways some rich dimensions of the developmental dynamics of faith. Before we turn to that task, however, let me provide a context and framework for our reflections.

PRELIMINARY ASSUMPTIONS

First, I make the assumption—or better, I have the conviction—that as part of the planfulness and intention manifest in creation, human beings are genetically potentiated for partnership with God. That is to say we are prestructured, as it were, to generate the capacities necessary for us as a species to fulfill our vocations as reflective-responsive members of creation. We have as part of our creatively evolved biological heritage the generative deep-structural tendencies that make possible our development as partners with one another and with God. With Saint Augustine we can affirm, "Thou hast made us for Thyself, and our hearts are restless until they find their rest in Thee."

Second, we must take seriously our talk about destiny, freedom, and fatedness, from the last chapter. I am suggesting here that part of our destiny as created and evolved beings is this genetic potentiation for reflective partnership with one another and with God. Potentiation, however, is not the same as realization. Deep-structuring potentials, as part of our destiny and freedom, can be thwarted and distorted by those dimensions of our destinies that result from the misuses of freedom by others that affect us, and from our own misuses of freedom. The same deep-structural potentials that make partnership with God possible can be developed and directed in the interactions of our living that constitute life, toward resistance to God and toward competition and defensiveness toward the neighbor. The genetically given capacities for faith and faithfulness toward

God, nature, and other human beings, which make us distinctly human, can be corrupted, misshaped, and misdirected.

Third, the context in which we become selves and form stances and styles of faith is community. There is no selfhood that is not formed in relation to others and to the culture of shared social meanings and institutions. Similarly, there is no faith that is not awakened and formed in the matrix of relationship, language, ritual, and symbol. In the practical theological effort to account for the dynamics of selfhood and faith by which we become subjects in relation to God, no individualistic psychologies or theologies can be of much help. Our effort to speak of the *praxis* of God required that we speak of a correlated *praxis* of human responsiveness. That effort led us to a theology that is dialectical in intent, that is to say, a theology that aims to bring to view the profound interaction of the human and the divine, and of creation and the divine. Similarly, the effort to capture the developmental dynamics of faith and selfhood requires that we make maximal effort to provide an interactionist, fully social account of our interrelatedness with God, creation, and the neighbor.

Fourth, the emergence of awareness, of reflective consciousness, and eventually of various kinds of self-reflectiveness, comes in humans as a gradual and difficult sequence of developmental constructions. To a large degree we begin as creatures embedded in nonconscious dependence upon, and interaction with, the environments that welcome us. Only gradually do we begin to differentiate ourselves as objects of awareness from the others and from the objects that constitute our environments. Even at the most developed levels, our critically reflective capacities for awareness and thought are highly selective functions of an organism that is part of an extraordinary ecology of organismic life. Most of our being, during most of our lives, is nonconscious and nonreflective; nonetheless, it is structured energy and action.

SELFHOOD AND FAITH

To be a self means, at the outset, to be a human being with structuring patterns that shape a distinctive style of being as a person. Selfhood depends in basic ways on our embodiment: we *are* our bodies. With embodiment comes a set of more or less integrated systems and functions that, largely without any conscious effort on our parts, constitute the remarkable concatenation of energy and animation that we call life or living. Embodiment brings with it certain ground rhythms. It brings a range of energy levels, an ease or difficulty of coordination, a bone structure and musculature with their indications of physical strength and endurance, and a facial mask with its particular range of expressive features. With embodiment there also comes another of the primary elements of self-hood: sexuality, erotic energies and needs, and the bases of gender iden- tity. To observe the unfolding, development, and ongoing change of bodies—our own and others'—is one of the fascinating dimensions of human life.

Embodiment, however, is but the beginning of selfhood. To be a self is a reflexive matter. It is a matter of becoming aware of self as self, and this means in relation to, and with the help of, the responses of others. A major concern of the stage theories we will elaborate in this chapter is with understanding the development of those capacities by which we construct self-other, self-self, and self-Ultimate or -God relations. As we trace the evolution of levels of social perspective taking in stages of selfhood and faith, we shall see how each new level affords enriched possibilities for knowledge of self and for intimacy with others and with God. We shall also attend to the various forms that self-deception takes at each of these stages. In this discussion we may be able to see how cunning and the capacity for evil to others have their own developmental histories as well.

In the embodied and reflexive self there forms a fundamental orienta- tion toward the conditions of existence. This fundamental orientation, like much of selfhood, constitutes a largely unreflective and unconscious disposition or stance. Only gradually and partially do we become aware of, capable of expressing, and intentional about shaping, the pervasive disposition we call faith. To call faith a disposition is to acknowledge that it involves both emotions and a kind of knowing or cognition. In the lan- guage of constructive-developmental psychologies, faith is a construing of the conditions of existence. It is a special kind of construing, however, for it attempts to make sense of our mundane everyday experience *in light of some accounting for the ultimate conditions of our existence.* In its efforts to orient us toward the ultimate conditions of existence, faith involves three impor- tant kinds of construal: (1) It involves a patterned knowing (which we sometimes call belief). (2) It involves a patterned valuing (which we some- times call commitment or devotion). And (3) it involves patterned con- structions of meaning, usually in the form of an underlying narrative or story.'

In constructive-developmental research and theory the focus of attention involves the patterns characterizing persons' construals of self-other, self-self, self-world, and self-Ultimate environment relations. The structuring underlying persons' selfhood and faith are identified by a kind of inference from the observation and analysis of certain kinds of behavior, including speech and self-description. Stages of selfhood and faith, in this perspective, refer to typical patterns of construal that we have come to understand as deriving from systematically integrated operations of knowing, valuing, and meaning construction. To speak of stages is to claim that these integrations of knowing, valuing, and meaning construction exhibit a certain formal uniformity in a range of persons. It is to claim that there is a developmental sequence of such systems of integrated operations. Further, it is to claim that the developmental sequence exhibits a series of qualitatively distinguishable patterns and that each pattern adds successively something qualitatively new and more complexly developed to the patterns that come before it.

STAGES OF SELFHOOD AND FAITH

In examining the following presentation of constructivist-developmental stages, our concern is to bring understanding to the process by which persons become subjects before and in relation to God and one another. We are trying to trace the interactional process by which the genetic potentials for partnership with God and the neighbor become activated and take form. In the presentation of these stages and in our discussions of them in subsequent chapters, we will attend to the strengths and limits of the operational structures of each stage. In no way will we be suggesting that a person characterized by one of the less developed stages is any less a person than one described by a more developed stage. Our concern, rather, will be to try to grasp the potentials and limits for the human vocation of covenant partnership with God and neighbor which are characteristic of each of the stages.

PRIMAL FAITH AND THE INCORPORATIVE SELF

We start our discussion of stages of faith and of ego development with a consideration of infancy. Faith and selfhood have their origins in us before birth, *in utero,* as we form in that most symbiotic of relationships the fetus has with its mother. We do not, of course, study intrauterine experience in the research we do. But it is difficult to see how prebirth experience could fail to make a fundamental contribution to the forming organic sense of self and environment. The environment of expectation surrounding the birth of a child is undoubtedly communicated to the infant through the emotional disposition of the mother, by biochemical as well as direct physical mediation. Prior to birth it seems likely that the child forms some sense of a welcoming and anticipatory cherishing or of its opposite.

In the twenty-minute passage through the birth canal, we almost smother. If the pregnancy has been normal, this is our first experience of the threat of negation or nonbeing. We gasp our way into relationship; we are squeezed and extruded into community. The responsiveness of this new environment, providing milk and the continuation of warmth and security, becomes coupled now with the hazy sights, sounds, and sensations of relation.

As we move into the world, faith begins with a kind of prelanguage disposition of trust and loyalty toward the environment into which we emerge. This trust and loyalty take form in the mutuality, the give-and-take, of the interactive rituals of relationship with those who provide our consistent primary care. Our rudimentary faith constructs "preimages" of powerful and trustworthy ultimacy, in order to offset the anxiety that results from the separations and the threats of negation that occur in the course of infantile development. Here we are dealing with what Erik Erikson describes as the tension between the development of basic trust and its struggle with basic mistrust.

Following both Freud and Piaget, Kegan has suggestively proposed that the baby's self consists in or is constituted by its reflexes, its sensing, its moving. In the infant's experience there is as yet no distinction between self and environment, or between self and those providing primary care. The baby, initially at least, experiences no subject-object distinction between mother, breast, swaddling clothes, bed, surrounding objects, and self. Because of the prestructured readiness to nurse (sucking reflex) and the sensitized readiness of the mouth to provide the first and most prominent link between the baby's needs and the environment's readiness to nurture, Kegan characterizes selfhood in this stage as that of the incorporative self. The infant is in this sense *all* subject, *all* experience. As yet there is no objective reality over against the infant; there is as yet no dualism of self-other, self-object, self-environment. Self and environment are one in the dim and fluid experience of the baby. We are embedded in our reflexes, our sensing, and our sensorimotor moving as infants.

During the first two years of life the infant undergoes a series of cognitive and relational separations or differentiations. These culminate in the child's having the ability to allow the mother and other primal caring persons to go away without undue stress and anxiety, because of the experience and internalized trust that the caretaker will return. During this time of steadily growing differentiation of the child from its environment, the presence and care of the mother or her substitute is crucial for mediating experiences of separation and return, and for the important "mirroring" that conveys deep regard and a clear focusing of self as "other" to the mother. Kegan calls these prerequisites for a strong rudimentary selfhood the "culture of mothering." If this culture is disrupted, especially in the first two years of life, the child is put at serious emotional risk.

INTUITIVE-PROJECTIVE FAITH
AND THE IMPULSIVE SELF

From about the time children begin to use language to communicate about self and objects in the world we see the emergence of a style of meaning-making we call the Intuitive-Projective stage. This stage represents an emotional and perceptual ordering of experience. Imagination, not yet disciplined by consistent logical operations, responds to story, symbol, dream, and experience. It attempts to form images that can hold and order the mixture of feelings and impressions evoked by the child's encounters with the newness of both everyday reality and the penumbra of mystery that surrounds and pervades it. Death emerges as a source of danger and mystery. Experiences of power and powerlessness orient children to a frequently deep existential concern about questions of security, safety, and the power of those upon whom they rely for protection. Owing to a naive egocentrism, children do not consistently differentiate their perspectives from those of others. Because of this lack of perspective taking, and in virtue of an as yet unreliable understanding of cause-and-effect relations, children construct and reconstruct events in episodic fashion. While appreciative of stories and capable of becoming deeply engrossed in them, they are seldom able to reconstruct very adequately the narrative pattern and detail of a story. The reconstructions they make take on an episodic quality, and in them fantasy and make-believe are not distinguished from factuality. Constructions of faith at this stage are drawn to symbols and images of visible power and size. There is an appreciation for stories that represent the powers of good and evil in unambiguous fashion.

These make it possible for children to symbolize the threatening urges and impulses that both fascinate and terrify them, while providing an identification with the vicarious triumphs of good over evil that stories—such as fairy tales—can provide. Curiously enough, symbols or representations of the deity at this stage may mix anthropomorphic and nonanthropomorphic imagery. There is in this stage the possibility of aligning powerful religious symbols and images with profound feelings of terror and guilt, as well as of love, ecstasy, and unity with the Ultimate. Such possibilities give this stage the potential for for ning deep-going and long-lasting emotional and imaginal orientations in faith—both for good and for ill.

What kind of selfhood correlates with this early stage of faith? Kegan names the style of selfhood at this stage the impulsive self. The child now has locomotor control and a workable integration of reflexes and sensorimotor coordination. He or she now "has" or controls the actions that were constitutive of the previous level of selfhood, that of the incorporative self. At the present stage, however, the child is embedded in—or constituted by—her or his impulses. The child, as far as emotions and self-control are concerned, does not *have* (in the sense of possess or control) impulses; rather, the child *is* its impulses. The child is constituted by—is embedded in—its logical fallacies, its egocentrism, its imagination, its perceptions, its internal contradictions of desire and fear of punishment. Tantrums, for example, are not something a four-y ar-old has. More appropriately we might say the tantrum has the four-year-old: he or she is internal to it. Tantrums are in a sense a logical expression of the impulsive child who is thwarted or frustrated by a world that he or she cannot fully interpret or make sense of.

We are our impulses at this stage. This means that we need what Kegan has called a "culture of parenting"—a culture that structures an environment in ways that provide dependable rituals and boundaries while allowing appropriate leeway for autonomy and experimentation. Such a parenting culture provides firm controls on our impulses and loving guidance in the internalization, without excessive harshness, of the controls of conscience. Kegan sees a yearning in this stage: a yearning to be overincluded in the love of one parent and for the exclusion from the loving relationship of the other parent. Part of what the parenting culture needs to provide at this stage is the presence of the other parent to contradict the child's yearning and, thereby, to protect the child from being emotionally swallowed up or devoured by the (temporarily) favored parent.

MYTHIC-LITERAL FAITH AND
THE IMPERIAL SELF

Somewhere between ages six and eight children typically undergo a revolution in the patterns of their thinking and valuing that open the way for a
new stage of faith and selfhood. The Mythic-Literal stage of faith rests
upon the emergence of new logical operations that make possible more
stable and dependable forms for shaping experience and meanings and of
conscious interpretation of them. Now cause-and-effect relations are
understood. Categories have been constructed for sorting out relations
and for grouping things into classes and types. A person now makes reliable distinctions between fantasy and make-believe, on the one hand, and
the data of empirical experience, on the other. In a dependable and taken-
for-granted way the young person is now capable of taking the perspectives of others on objects or events of their common interest. Children now
construct their experience world in terms of a new linearity and predictability. The constructions and understandings of this stage, however, are
marked by concreteness, literalness, and one-dimensionality of meanings. While capable of responding to and being affected by symbols and
their multiple layers of meanings, the Mythic-Literal stage does not repro-
duce or consciously interpret abstractions or the many nuances of symbol
or myth. This combination of factors gives rise to one of the most striking
features of the Mythic-Literal stage: its orientation to narrative and story
as the principal means of constructing, conserving, and sharing meanings.

Though children of preschool age enjoy and are deeply informed by
stories, it is those of school age who become virtuoso storytellers and story
creators. The narrative structuring of experience that emerges in this
stage provides a central way of establishing identity, through the learning
of the stories of those groups and communities to which one belongs. Similarly, in the absence yet of the ability to reflect upon the self as a
personality—something about which I will say more in due course—
persons of this stage share who they are by telling stories of their experiences and belonging. At this point, however, persons of Mythic-Literal
faith do not have the ability to step outside the flowing streams of their
stories and experiences in order to reflect upon them and draw overarch-
ing meanings from them. At this stage they do not yet construct an integrative "story of their stories."

Because of the ability to take the perspectives of others, this stage orients to the simple but important form of justice contained in equality and moral reciprocity. Fairness consists in treating like cases alike: "You scratch my back and I'll scratch yours," etc. One sees and knows that others have interests, needs, and goals different from one's own. In order to secure the cooperation of others, our bargaining must take their interests and needs into account. Fair is fair.

This imperative of moral reciprocity provides the intuitive basis for a construction of God, and of God's dealing with the world, that is very typical of Mythic-Literal faith. In this construction, God is seen in anthropomorphic terms on the order of a stern, powerful, but just parent or ruler. God rewards people when they do right; God punishes people when they do wrong. Taken on a cosmic scale, this results in the kind of interpretation that looks at the world, in the words of an engineer friend of mine, as a "quick pay-off universe." It is of a piece with the cause-and-effect, concrete narrative sort of construction of meanings which emerges with such power in this stage.

This stage as yet lacks something very important that will come with later stages: it lacks the ability to understand its own interiority—its own pervasive dispositions, the sources of its wishes, the structure of its motives, the patterns of its personality. What it does not know about itself it is hardly able to penetrate in others: persons of the Mythic-Literal stage lack the ability to construct the interiority of other persons, as well. This means that from within the patterns of knowing and valuing of this stage, persons are seen as rounded, moving, behaving surfaces. The behaviorism of B. F. Skinner represents a complex and sophisticated attempt to account for the possibility of understanding and predicting the behavior of organisms—including human organisms—from a standpoint that knows nothing of the interiority of persons. This lack represents no real problem in dealing with children of elementary-school age, where this orientation typically takes form. But in adolescents or adults—among whom it is not unusual to find persons who are typified by this stage—it makes for rather more difficult problems of understanding and response. Kegan's discussion of this stage in selfhood helps us at this point.

Kegan describes the selfhood that correlates with the Mythic-Literal stage as that of the imperial self. Why does he call it by that name? It is because selfhood in this stage is embedded in its needs, wishes, and interests. By "embedded in" I mean that the self is constituted, in terms of its behavior and motivation, by its needs, wishes, and interests, and the self does not examine those needs, wishes, and interests. They are simply there, and they motivate one's behaviors and responses without one's being reflective about their power. At this stage one is not constituted any longer by impulse—one *has* one's impulses, and has them in control. At this stage, however, one *is* one's structure of needs, wishes, and interests. One does not see these things about the self. Rather, one sees the world, self, and others through the structure of one's needs, wishes, and interests: they become the filters shaping a persons's interpretations of experience and other persons. Persons typified by this stage—especially those of adolescent age or beyond—we often experience as manipulative, because they often seem to act so as to get our behavior and responses to serve their interests, needs, and wishes. What is not so clear with older examples of the imperial self, however, is that we are not in fact dealing with conscious and calculating manipulation based on a shrewd appraisal of our internal structure of motivations. Rather, we are dealing with a more naive and honest form of manipulation carried on by those who see us only as rounded surfaces whose behavior has to be predicted, if at all, on the basis of the pattern of responses we make to sometimes crude forms of stimulation and challenge.

The yearning of the imperial self Kegan sees as a longing for a certain kind of independence rooted in self-esteem and competence. If I can do things well, if I have competence, I will be recognized as one who can be self-directing and not subject to the guidance of others. The culture of support needed by this stage, Kegan suggests, is one of family and school, where the imperial self can be kept in check by loving restraint and where ongoing relations of trust and care make it possible to begin to attend reflectively to the deeper sources and patterns of motivation and personality in self and others.

SYNTHETIC-CONVENTIONAL FAITH AND THE INTERPERSONAL SELF

Between the ages of eleven and thirteen, typically, another revolution in the operations of knowing and valuing can occur. This is an age when the capacities for abstract thinking and for the manipulation of concepts can begin to form. The emergence of these new kinds of thinking has implications for the development of selfhood and faith at a number of levels. At the heart of the transition to the Synthetic-Conventional stage of faith is a dramatic new capability in social perspective taking. In the previous stage, perspective taking was limited largely to making allowances for the fact that others see and experience objects of common interest from their own positions and perspectives. It was understood that if one is to communicate successfully with others, account must be taken of such differences in onlook. This kind of simple perspective taking makes it possible to tell stories in responsible ways or to write letters to friends and strangers—both of these being tasks that require construction of the perspectives of our audiences or correspondents.

With the revolution of knowing that can come with adolescence, however, a quantum leap into a whole new dimension of social perspective taking can occur. This is called mutual interpersonal perspective taking. Here is the way it develops: Either in a chum relationship between persons of the same or opposite sex or in a first-love or "puppy love" tie, the young person finds another with whom there is trust, regard, and excitement enough to spend long hours in conversation and in a kind of mirroring communication and exchange. In this process the young person, frequently for the first time, finds a depth of relation with a nonfamily member in which he or she can see the self reflectively—and this precisely at a time of coming to terms with the often explosive physiological and emotional changes that adolescence brings. In such a relationship the youth experiences what I have found possible to sum up in a couplet:

> I see you seeing me:
> I see the me I think you see.

Here one has the novel and exciting experience of beginning to construct an image of the self one sees others seeing. One begins to try to compose the self-image that mediates between what one feels oneself to be and what a significant other—or others—seems to be mirroring back. Here we can plainly recognize the basis, in knowing and valuing, of what Erik Erikson has called the "identity crisis."[8]

In time, the youth recognizes that the other also experiences a mirroring in their relationship. It becomes clear that in a kind of reciprocal way he or she is serving as a means whereby the companion is also able to compose an image of self inspired by their communication. The youth recognizes, vis-a-vis the other, that

> You see you according to me:
> You see the you you think I see.

A genuinely new kind of self-awareness results from these early experiences of mutual interpersonal perspective taking. In having access to others' images of oneself, one is stimulated to reflect on one's present feelings and self-awareness. This kind of reflection can then be focused on one's memories and on the personal past, leading to a reconstrual of many previous experiences on the basis of new operations of thought and interpretation. Similarly, with the new cognitive operations available to the youth, it is possible (and necessary) to begin thinking about the projection of the self into possible futures. Now, in ways the Mythical-Literal stage never allowed, one begins to assemble the composite meanings of one's stories—to form a story of one's stories. Through such reflection and constructions one begins to be aware of and attend to one's own interiority and that of others.

As mutual interpersonal perspective taking becomes a dependable and consistent acquisition, the young person becomes acutely attuned to the evaluative expectations and responses of a circle of significant others. These may include peers of a variety of sorts, parents, teachers, representatives of a religious community, and the more "generalized others" made salient through the media or street culture. This variety of significant others mirrors the becoming self in different and sometimes tension-filled ways. The task of this stage is to synthesize into a workable unity a sense of identity based on the range of images of self provided by those who matter. This forming unity must also integrate the sense of self derived from internal feelings and reflections on the self's present, past, and future.

Corresponding to the struggle to form into a workable unity a sense of identity, the youth must also pull into a synthesis values, beliefs, and allegiances that will support and confirm her or his sense of identity. Such commitments play a central role in the unification of a sense of self. Promise making and promise keeping constitute foundational ways in which a now-reflective self forms identity. One might more adequately say *conforms* an identity, for in fact it is a *forming-with* others through shared commitments and loyalties. This conforming quality of the synthesis of faith at this stage is what leads us to describe it as conventional.

In this stage, personality, both as style and as substance, becomes an absorbing concern. Values, commitments, and relationships are seen as central to identity and worth, at a time when worth is heavily keyed to the approval and affirmation of significant others. This stage holds together a vital but fragile dance in which youths try to shape the movements of their lives to give expression to a way of being that is forming from within, at the same time trying to maintain connections and exchanges with all those to whom their becoming seems integrally related. This strong need to maintain connections with and meet the expectations of the significant others can become in Sharon Parks's phrase the "tyranny of the *they*." Such overconformity to internalized or external "others" is in adults what David Riesman called "other-directedness."[9]

The beliefs and values linking youths with their range of significant others take form in a tacit, largely unexamined unity. From within this stage persons tend to construct the ultimate environment in terms of the personal. God is one who knows us better than we can know ourselves. God knows who we are and who we are becoming, and can be counted on as friend, companion, lifeline, or Divine Other to sustain and fulfill our selfhood. Typically, within this stage persons have the deep feeling that in connecting mutuality with others and with ourselves we are somehow linked with the depth, or height, of ultimacy.

Selfhood in this stage is acutely attuned to the realm of the interpersonal. In calling this the interpersonal self Kegan calls attention to the ways in which persons best described by this stage manifest an embeddedness in the world of interpersonal mutuality. We can say with truth of this stage, whether seen in adolescence or later adulthood, that the self is constituted by its relationships and its roles: "I *am* my relationships; I *am* my roles." Being embedded in the interpersonal means that the self is a derivative of its interpersonal relatedness. There is not as yet a self that *has* roles and relations without being fully identical with or fully expressed by them. The self, rather, is a function of its significant social ties.

As we will see in a subsequent chapter, the persons best described by Synthetic-Conventional faith often feel an unrecognized ambivalence about their dependence on others for the sustainment of identity and faith. On the one hand, there is an awareness of dependence and the paramount importance of connectedness. On the other hand, there is a usually unrecognized resentment of the fact of this dependence and of the "tyranny of the they" to the extent that it is present. In this stage, Kegan points out, one is deeply dependent upon a culture of interpersonal mutuality. If key relations end or central roles collapse or are lost, persons of this stage are put at serious risk. The central yearning of this stage in both selfhood and faith is for inclusion as a form of intimacy. This desire for inclusion makes conflict with significant others or community difficult and threatening. It is a form of intimacy that runs the risk of an interpersonal fusion of personal boundaries.

INTERLUDE

We have come a fair distance in examining some of the development dynamics of selfhood and faith. Our concern has been to draw upon constructive-developmental theory and research to provide a framework for understanding the movement of selves, by way of struggle from stage to stage, toward realization of their potentiation for increasingly conscious, increasingly aware and responsible partnership with God.

In the description of these stages of faith and selfhood, I have given typical ages of onset for the transition to each stage. Reading between the lines, however, reveals that there is nothing inevitable or automatic about transition from one of these stages to another. The Mythic-Literal stage and the imperial self not only describe the structuring of faith and selfhood of many children of elementary-school age, but their features can also be found in many adolescents and adults. There are minimum ages under which it would be unusual to find a person in a particular stage. For example, it would be unusual to find a person well into the Synthetic-Conventional stage before early adolescence, or well into the Individuative-Reflective stage before the twenties. But transitions to those stages can come much later or for some persons not at all.

By now I hope it is clear that we are trying to describe the underlying patterns of knowing, valuing, and committing that constitute persons' ways of being selves and in faith. We are not, except by occasional example, describing the contents of persons' faith and identity. To link this with the beginning of the chapter: we are trying to trace the development, through persons' interactions with the conditions in which life places them, of those genetic potentials for the vocation of covenant partnership with God that come with creation. We are tracing the path by which persons in community become subjects before God and increase in their capacities for self-aware, self-critical, and responsible partnership with God.

We come now to examine the transition to a stage that in important ways parallels in individual lives and communities something of what intellectual elites in Europe and North America struggled with in that watershed period we call the Enlightenment. The personal and communal recapitulation of that cultural transition in contemporary society and communities carries the same kinds of exhilaration and dangers and the same kinds of potentials for both liberation and self-deception that the original period manifested.

INDIVIDUATIVE-REFLECTIVE
FAITH AND THE
INSTITUTIONAL SELF

This stage we find emerging only in young adulthood or beyond. Transition to this stage requires breaking up the balance of the Synthetic-Conventional stage's dance. Specifically, two important movements must occur, together or in sequence. First, the previous stage's tacit system of beliefs, values, and commitments must be critically examined. This means that persons must undergo a sometimes painful disruption of their deeply held but unexamined world view or belief system. The familiar and taken-for-granted must be made strange. The assumptive configuration of meanings assembled to support their selfhood in its roles and relations must now be allowed to become problematic. Evocative symbols and stories by which lives have been oriented will now be critically questioned and interpreted. So the first movement involves disembedding from the previous stage's assumptive and tacitly held system of beliefs and values. Second, the self, previously constituted and sustained by its roles and relationships, must struggle with the question of identity and worth apart from its previously defining connections. This does not mean that the relations have to be broken. Nor does it mean that the roles must be relinquished. Rather, it means that persons must take into themselves much of the authority they previously invested in others for determining and sanctioning their goals and values. It means that definitions of the self dependent upon roles and relationships with others must now be regrounded in terms of a new quality of responsibility that the self takes for defining itself and orchestrating its roles and relations.

At the heart of this double movement in the transition to the Individuative-Reflective stage is a new development in social perspective taking. It begins with the construction of what we call a third-person perspective. In the acute attunement to the expectations and evaluations of significant others that marks the movement to the Synthetic-Conventional stage and to interpersonal selfhood, persons depend at first upon external relations for confirmation and support of the self. Gradually, in that stage the expectations and conforming judgments of valued others become an internalized part of one's personality. These internalized "voices" of significant others provide guidance and constraint for the interpersonal self. When external or internalized authorities conflict, however, or when their tutelage becomes cramping or constrictive for a developing person, the self must construct a perspective from which both self and the relations with others can be seen from beyond the embeddedness in interpersonal relations. The third-person perspective provides an angle of vision from which evaluations of the expectations of others can be made and from which conflicting claims or expectations can be adjudicated. The use of the third-person perspective provides a basis for claiming one's own authority. It provides a basis from which assessments and choices can be made in relation to the beliefs, values, and elements of life style one has evolved.

This description makes the generation and employment of the third-person perspective sound easy. As later discussion will show, however, there frequently is considerable internal emotional resistance to relinquishing or pushing away from the reliance on the authority of others. There is considerable concern about whether altering relationships of dependence will necessarily mean an ending of the relationships. In the case of internalized "voices from behind us" there is often a feeling of having "broken faith" with our betters—those whose examples and teachings were of central importance in getting us launched as selves and as persons of faith. As we develop some distance and capacity to decide about the power of others' expectations in the governance of our lives, we are also likely to feel a fear of the loss of the self. Or if we give up definitions of ourselves derived from the roles we play, we probably are going to feel some measure of anxiety about whether there will still be a self. And if a person is beyond young adulthood there is a whole network of relationships in which her or his membership is grounded in mutual or reciprocal dependence upon shared values, beliefs, and life patterns. To disrupt that network by claiming a qualitatively new authority for one's life and by critically examining shared beliefs and values is likely to feel, both to the person and to her or his circle of relations, like an abandonment of community.

In this qualitatively new kind of authority and responsibility for oneself and one's outlook, one begins to be able to answer the question, Who are you when you are not defined by being so-and-so's daughter or son or so-and-so's wife or husband? One faces the question, Who are you when you are not defined by that occupational or professional role or by that circle of friendships and belonging? Whereas previously the self was derivative of its roles and relations, now a self is being claimed and constituted which *has* roles and relations but is not exhaustively identified with any of them. In the emergence of what I call an executive ego, and Kegan calls the institutional self, there begins to be the sense of a self that is in charge of the many selves one is. Now there is an "I" that orchestrates the roles one plays and the relations one has but that is not identical with any of them. In the celebration of this executive "I" a person becomes concerned about clarity of the boundaries of personal identity. One becomes concerned that there should be congruence, authenticity, and fit between one's clarified identity, one's chosen membership affiliations, and one's espoused beliefs and values. This focuses the question of the critical examination of one's heritage of beliefs, symbols, and values.

The Enlightenment represented a movement in cultural evolution where inherited symbols, beliefs, and traditions were subjected to the scrutiny and evaluation of critical reasoning. Similarly, the development of the Individuative-Reflective stage of faith involves the critical examination and exercise of choice regarding a person or community's previous faith perspectives. In many respects this is a "demythologizing" stage. Creeds, symbols, stories, and myths from religious traditions are likely to be subjected to analysis and to translation to conceptual formulations. In this process there are both gains and losses. Meanings previously taken on authority and allowed to inform faith in emotionally powerful but intellectually unexamined ways now are made explicit and systematic. This process brings gains in clarity, precision, and the sorting out of what is defensible from that which is not. But there are losses too. Paul Tillich pointed out that a symbol that is recognized as a symbol no longer has the power of a symbol. The powerful participation of a symbol in that which it symbolizes, which makes it possible for the symbol to mediate relationship with its reality, is now broken. While the conceptual analysis and translation of the symbol make its meanings explicit, we may fail to notice that in the process of communicating meanings the initiative has shifted from the symbol to the analyst of the symbol.

The control of meanings implicit in what I have just described joins with the control of the self and its boundaries we examined earlier, in the full realization of Individuative-Reflective faith and the institutional self. In a way that parallels the impact of the Enlightenment, persons can fall into a kind of self-deception based on the illusion of a more complete control of themselves and of the conditions of their existence than in fact will prove to be the case. In its confidence that it has retained the essential from its religious traditions, the Individuative-Reflective stage is likely to fall victim to its own reductionism. In its more self-certain forms this stage gives rise not to individuation but to individualism. Kegan's discussion of the institutional self helps us see that this stage involves claiming oneself as the author of one's life. It puts a premium on self-dependence and self-ownership. Its culture of support and embeddedness is that of achieved identity and self-authorization. It is placed at risk when the largely unacknowledged bases for its overconfidence become shaken. This can happen when the self, working so hard to maintain its explicit meanings and firm, clear boundaries, begins to come to terms with loneliness, vulnerability, and the limits to an intimacy based upon self-sponsorship and control. Or it may come when the self, confident in its self-authorship, is confronted by the fact of its massive embeddedness in and dependence upon a complex of systems that it can never control. Or it may come when the conscious self, overconfident in its illusions of self-knowledge and control, must begin to acknowledge depths of unrecognized hungers, voices of inspiration and guidance, and sources of disruption in the unconscious which begin to insist upon inclusion. These kinds of experience and awareness do not usually emerge before the edge of midlife—the mid-thirties or beyond. Some persons manage to avoid having them ever emerge. When they do begin to impinge upon a person's consciousness he or she is poised at the point of possible transition to another stage of faith and selfhood.

CONJUNCTIVE FAITH AND THE
INTER-INDIVIDUAL SELF

The name for the Conjunctive stage of faith implies a rejoining or a union of that which previously has been separated. I take the name from Nicolas of Cusa (1401–64) who wrote about what he called the *coincidentia oppositorum*, the "coincidence of opposites," in our apprehensions of truth. The confident clarity about the boundaries of self and faith which the previous stage worked so hard to achieve must be relinquished in the move to the Conjunctive stage. Carlyle Marney spoke about this transition in our lives when he, in an autobiographical reference to a time when he had a heart attack at the peak of his powers, said, "And I developed an ego-leak." The executive ego, which claims authority for its own decisions and which selectively affirms values and beliefs that it finds acceptable, must come to terms with the fact that its confidence is based in part at least on illusion or upon seriously incomplete self-knowledge. We are many selves: we *have* a conscious mind, but we also *are* a great deal of patterned action and reaction that is largely unconscious. Those powerful and important unconscious aspects of selfhood are both personal and social in origin. Perhaps, in Jungian terms, there are archetypal contents in the unconscious as well. We are driven and pushed from underneath by motives, desires, hungers—and lures of the spirit—which we have difficulty recognizing and integrating. Yet we have to come to terms with them, for they shape and sometimes distort our behavior; they limit our capacities to be responsible selves.

In the transition to Conjunctive faith one begins to make peace with the tension arising from the fact that truth must be approached from a number of different directions and angles of vision. As part of honoring truth, faith must maintain the tensions between these multiple perspectives and refuse to collapse them in one direction or another. In this respect, faith begins to come to terms with dialectical dimensions of experience and with apparent paradoxes: God is both immanent and transcendent; God is both an omnipotent and a self-limiting God; God is the sovereign of history while being the incarnate and crucified One. In physics, in order to account for the behavior of light, two incompatible and unintegrable models must be employed—one based on the analogy with packets of energy, and the other upon the analogy with wavelike motions somewhat as in sound. Similarly, many truthful theological insights and models involve holding together in dialectical tension the "coincidence of opposites."

As regards faith and its expression in this stage, we must speak of a kind of epistemological humility. The Conjunctive stage recognizes that properly we stutter when we speak of the Divine. The reality our symbols and metaphors seek to bring to expression both spills over them in excess and recedes behind them in a simultaneous disclosure and concealment of the holy. Notably, the Conjunctive stage marks a movement beyond the demythologizing strategy of the Individuative stage. Where the latter followed the Enlightenment's tendency to reduce the symbolic and metaphoric to conceptual translations, this new state reverses the flow of initiative. Acknowledging the multidimensionality and density of symbols and myth, persons of the Conjunctive stage learn in new ways to submit to their initiative and mediating power: instead of "reading" and analyzing the symbols and metaphors, they learn to submit to the "reading" and illumination of their situations which these and other elements of tradition offer. In what Paul Ricoeur has called a "second" or "willed" naiveté, the Conjunctive stage manifests a readiness to enter into the rich dwellings of meaning which true symbols, liturgy, and parable offer.[10] Faith learns in this stage to be receptive, to balance initiative and control with waiting and seeking in order to be a part of the larger movement of spirit or being.

Another central feature of Conjunctive faith is its orientation to the "stranger." Partly because of its acknowledgment of the stranger within and partly because of its recognition of the relativity of place, language, and culture of its own apprehensions in faith, the Conjunctive stage learns to bring a principled openness to encounters with the strange truths of other religious and cultural traditions. I do not here speak of a wishy-washy sense of openness in which one has no strongly held convictions. Rather, I refer precisely to its opposite. Conjunctive faith, attuned to paradox and the tensional dialectic between religious symbols and common human experience, leads to a readiness for serious and mutual dialogue with traditions other than its own. It is confident that new depths and corrected perceptions of the truths of its own tradition can be the result.

While ready to make assessments and critical evaluations of the truth claims of other traditions, this stage is also ready to invite and consider similar assessments and evaluations of its own faith stance made by responsible representatives of those other traditions. This stage has little use for the narrow tribalism of homogeneous religious groupings or for the chauvinism of ideological holy war. Persons in this stage do have deep and particular convictions that account for their nondefensiveness in the dialogue with other traditions or perspectives.

Kegan refers to the self of this stage as the inter-individual self. No longer embedded in the executive ego, this stage *has* an ego. Its embeddedness comes in the constitution of the self, and its meanings in the impingement of multiple cultural and institutional systems and in the meanings they generate and maintain. This experience of the pull and tension of multiple perspectives marks an essential dynamic of the Conjunctive stage in selfhood—its holding together of several great polar tensions in selfhood and experience. In this stage one must come to terms with being both old and young. One of the peculiar dimensions of the experience of midlife and beyond is the strange mixture of continuity and sameness with one's own earlier and younger self, combined with the unmistakable and powerful signals that one has entered quite different seasons. In a second major polarity, one must incorporate recognitions that one is not only a constructive and well-meaning person but that one is also—often without intending it—a destructive person. In interdependences, of which we may only gradually and partially become aware, our very beings impinge on others in ways that bring them pain or bring us benefit from the diminishment of their life chances. A third set of polar tensions derives from our coming to terms with our being both masculine and feminine creatures or with our having to integrate in a new balance aspects of the cultural meanings of our own and the opposite sex. Finally, there is the polarity of finding that we are both conscious and unconscious selves and that the hidden aspects and movements of the self must be acknowledged and taken account of.

Readiness for a different quality of intimacy marks the person of Conjunctive faith. On the one hand, he or she struggles toward the awareness of a personal uniqueness and singularity that comes with genuine individuation: he or she is no longer identical with social roles and expectations, nor is he or she driven to the same extent as previously by unexamined hungers and motives. On the other hand, he or she has a heightened sense of interdependence and solidarity with the stranger without and within, and with the human generally. We are digged out of the same pit, and we are subject to the same range of flaws, foibles, cussedness, and glory. If real intimacy involves a closeness with that which is *other* to the self, without the need either to dominate it or to flee, then the Conjunctive stage should bring a readiness and taste for such relatedness. This manifests itself in a concern to connect with persons and classes different from the self; it shows up in a principled openness to the challenging truths of those who are religious or ideological "strangers"; and it leads in the direction of a deepened quality of spirituality in which one hungers for ways to relate to the otherness in self, God, and fellow humans.

UNIVERSALIZING FAITH AND THE GOD-GROUNDED SELF

Through the use of constructive-developmental theories of faith and selfhood we are trying to account for some of the processes through which human beings grow into their vocations as reflective members of nature and history. We are tracing a path of increasing self-awareness and capacity for both critical consciousness of and imaginative participation in the actions and intentions of God.

We come now to the last stage we are aware of in this process. I call it the

Universalizing stage of faith. Kegan does not deal with this stage. In the interest of symmetry and descriptiveness, however, I shall speak of the stage of selfhood that goes with Universalizing faith as that of the God-grounded self.

In this stage we see persons moving beyond the paradoxical awareness and the embrace of polar tensions of the Conjunctive stage. The structuring of the Universalizing stage derives from the radical completion of a process of decentration from self that we have been tracing throughout the sequence of stages. From the adualism of the infant and Primal faith, and the egocentrism of the Intuitive-Projective stage, we have seen a steady widening in social perspective taking as we have considered each subsequent stage. Gradually the circle of "those who count" in the meanings of faith and selfhood expands, until at the Conjunctive stage it extends well beyond the bounds of social class, nation, race, ideological affinity, and religious tradition. In Universalizing faith this process comes to a kind of completion. In the previous stage, despite an openness to the stranger and despite a commitment to a commonwealth of love and justice beyond any of our present communities, persons continue to live in the tension between the inclusiveness and transformation of their visions toward a new ultimate order and their rootedness in and loyalties to their segment of the existing order. The Conjunctive self is a tensional self.

With those persons who are drawn beyond the Conjunctive into the Universalizing stage of faith we seem to see a movement in which the self is drawn beyond itself into a new quality of participation and grounding in God, or the Principle of Being. In the completion of the process of decentration from self, with this stage the self is no longer the prime reference point from which the knowing and valuing of faith are carried out. Figure and ground are reversed: where previously the self was apprehended as a figure interposed upon the (back)ground of Being, now self is relinquished as epistemological and axiological center. To say it more simply, with the Universalizing stage, persons are drawn toward an identification with God in which the bases of identity, knowing (epistemology), and valuing (axiology) are transformed. There is a relinquishing of self into the ground of Being, a kind of reversal of figure and ground in which the person of faith now participates, albeit as a finite creature, in a kind of identification with God's way of knowing and valuing other creatures. In this sort of perspective those whom one has experienced as enemies come to be seen transformingly as God's children who must be loved radically and redemptively. This kind of transvaluation of valuing gives rise to strategies of nonviolent opposition to entrenched evil in hearts and societies. It gives rise to activist efforts, through the pouring out of the self, to transform present social conditions in the direction of God's commonwealth of love and justice.

Decentered persons manifest the fruits of a powerful kind of *kenosis* or emptying of self which is the fruit of having one's affections, one's love, powerfully drawn beyond the finite centers of value and power that bid to offer us meaning and security.

From the standpoint of a Christian understanding of the future that God intends in creation, governance, and liberation and redemption, we may describe such persons as colonists of the kingdom of God. Because of hearts and wills that have become vitally connected with the Divine Spirit, they live as though God's commonwealth of love and justice were already a decisive reality among us. As such, they constitute both transforming and critically challenging presences among us. In them we see the human being in some approximation of its fullness and completion, and we are drawn to it. At the same time, in relation to them we see the compromises, numbness, and enmity toward God's future that mark the social and personal patterns of our lives, and we are repelled.

What kind of self is this? Kegan does not help us here. I believe that the self in this stage is, in a radical sense, regrounded beyond itself in God. I am not talking about moral perfection here, nor am I speaking of perfect psychic balance or integration. Persons of universalizing faith continue to be finite creatures with blind spots, inconsistencies, and distorted capacities for relatedness to others. But I am talking about a selfhood that transfers the burden of self-integration and self-justification radically into God, and therefore has a new quality of freedom with the self and with others. The God-grounded self moves beyond the structuring of the world and others from the self's perspective, that is, as a meeting place of systems, of ideologies and relations. This self moves beyond usual forms of defensiveness and exhibits an openness based on groundedness in the being, love, and regard of God. I think that the yearning of this stage, insofar as I have any sense of it, is that all creation should be complete and that all God's creatures should be one. The vision, in New Testament terms, is of the messianic banquet where all will be seated together in the glory of God's presence, where wounds will be healed and enmities resolved, and where there will be food enough for everyone. What is arresting about these persons of Universalizing faith and God-grounded selfhood is that in quiet or in public ways they live as though the kingdom of God were already a realized fact among us. They thereby create zones of liberation and redemption in the world which are both threatening and freeing to the rest of us.

CHAPTER 5

The Congregation: Varieties of Presence in Selfhood and Faith

In presenting the stages of faith to groups including pastors, Christian educators, and clinicians over the last several years, I have found repeatedly that I am not presenting something totally new to them. Most savvy practitioners of ministry have already constructed, as part of what Michael Polanyi might call their tacit knowing, something resembling a developmental theory of faith and selfhood. Experience and reflection have led them to recognize differences in the ways persons compose and express their meanings. On the other hand, their teaching and living with the sources of faith in Scripture and tradition have led them to form more or less determinate images of maturity or fullness in faith and selfhood. For these reasons I recognize that faith-development theory and its theological elaboration in practical theology are neither alien nor necessarily new for persons in ministry. Instead, they offer an opportunity for practitioners to make their own observations and insights more explicit, and to bring to more specific and conscious awareness the elements of their own practical theologies of pastoral care and nurture in faith.

This chapter is designed to mediate between the theoretical account of stages of faith and selfhood given in chapter 4 and the pastor's experience of persons in and beyond the congregation. Here I want to provide characterizations and observations that can help us recognize when we are in the presence of persons best described by one or other of the stages or transitions presented in the developmental theories. The intent of this chapter is to provide a practical guide to pastoral diagnostics based on chapter 4's presentation of Kegan's and my work. As I attempt to sketch recognizable features of each of the stages, I will offer suggestions about implications of these descriptions for the provision of pastoral care.

In what follows I am indebted to the work of Carl Schneider[1] and Steven

S. Ivy.[2] Both of these pastoral clinicians have made important contributions to marshaling faith development theory as a diagnostic framework for pastoral care. Ivy's account has combined faith development theory with Kegan's account of stages of selfhood. I have been stimulated and informed by the work of both these men. Neither of them, however, can be held responsible for my efforts here to lay down the ground lines of a practical approach to pastoral identification of probable stages and transitions in members of groups in the congregation. Moreover, the informal and impressionistic criteria I am offering here are in no measure a substitute for the use of the *Manual for Faith Development Research*, which is now available for guiding rigorous social-scientific research. Nor are the kinds of observation and informal inventory taking I offer here substitutes for the extensive and probing faith-development interview by which accurate assessments of faith stages are made. Similarly, the working descriptions of stages of faith and selfhood in this chapter are not adequate to make the kinds of assessments upon which Kegan's theory of the evolving self is grounded. Nonetheless, if used with care and thoughtfulness, these depictions can provide significant help in guiding preaching, in informing the conduct of groups in spiritual direction and faith growth, in the work of healing and transitional support in personal or group pastoral counseling, and in the planning of educational programs and approaches.

Before laying out the stage-related styles of congregational presence, I must mention four cautions. First, it is a paramount concern of mine that the stages of faith and selfhood never be used for purposes of nefarious comparison or the devaluing of persons. Properly used, the stage theories should facilitate our understanding of persons whose ways of being in faith may differ significantly from our own. The theories should provide frameworks for seeing persons and their differences more clearly and less judgmentally or defensively.

Second, these are not to be understood as stages in soteriology. There is no sense in which a person must have constructed a given stage of development in faith or selfhood in order to be "saved." It is certainly possible to point to persons of serenity, courage, and genuine faith commitment who would be described—even as adults—in terms of any stage from Intuitive Projective to Universalizing.

Third, it is not necessarily the goal of pastoral care or counseling that employs developmental perspectives to try to propel or impel persons from one stage to another. Of course there is a normativity to the developmental theories we have introduced in the last chapter. Other things being equal, persons should be supported and encouraged to continue to engage the issues of their lives and vocations in such ways that development will be a likely result. Pastoral care will seek to involve them in disciplines and actions, in struggle and reflection, that will keep their faith and vocations responsive to the ongoing call of God. But we must remember that developmental stage transition is a complex and often protracted affair. Transitions cannot and should not be rushed. Development takes time. Much of our concern in pastoral care has to do with helping persons extend the operations of a given stage to the full range of their experiences and interactions. Integration and reconfiguration of memories, beliefs, and relationships in the light of the operations which a new stage makes possible are every bit as important as supporting, encouraging, and pacing persons in the move from one stage to another.

Fourth and finally, it probably is not helpful to think of stage transition or development from one stage to another as the direct goal of pastoral care, preaching, or Christian education. Our first concern, of course, is the proclamation of the gospel and the attempt to help it find a deep and firm rooting in the soil of people's lives. Next we are concerned about the awakening and shaping of vocation in accordance with an understanding of partnership with the action of God. If we are faithful in the pastoral leadership relating to these tasks, faith development, as a movement from one stage to another, will come as byproduct and fruit of our common work and that of the Spirit.

My interest now is exceedingly practical: How can a thoughtful pastor or educator discern when he or she is in the presence of an adult best described by the Mythic-Literal stage of faith? What clues suggest that one is interacting with a person of Individuative-Reflective faith? How do we recognize a transitional person dealing with the movement from the Synthetic-Conventional to the Individuative stage? Alongside questions of recognition and identification we must give attention to what these stage characteristics imply for preaching, counseling, teaching, spiritual direction, and doing organizational work with persons of different and transitional places. Finally, there are questions that derive from trying to understand and relate to groups in which persons of several stages may be interacting. How does "cross-stage static" manifest itself in the tensions and struggles of group life? Do congregations or subcongregations have *modal developmental levels*—that is, average expectable levels of development for adults? If so, how do the presence and pressures of this modal level affect the common life, decision making, and pastoral care of a congregation? If a congregation strives to understand itself and operate as a "public church" communion, what stage or stages must inform its work of pastoral care and the development of its ecology of care and vocation? With these questions urging us on, let us examine the visible characteristics of typical persons at the various developmental stages of faith and selfhood.

VARIETIES OF CONGREGATIONAL PRESENCE

Any time a pastor or priest greets a congregation of any real size gathered for worship, he or she addresses persons whose range of stages of faith and selfhood includes at least three or four stages. In addition to being an ecology of care and vocation, the congregation is an ecology of multiple stages of faith and selfhood. In a typical service of worship the clergy leads the congregation in one liturgy, with one sequence of prayers, one creedal affirmation, one set of Scripture readings, one offering of the Eucharist, and one sermon or homily. But because the congregation represents a pluralism of stages of faith and selfhood, that experience is subject to constructive interpretation in distinctively different modes. From young to old, from the Intuitive-Projective to the Conjunctive stage or beyond, participants make sense of what is going on in that service in a variety of systematically different ways. Preachers know this from the comments people make after their sermons: sometimes one recognizes what a listener names as having been so helpful from the sermon; at other times one does not. The listener constructs the meanings in accordance with the particular set of experiences, needs, hopes, and beliefs which he or she brings to the service, to be sure. But the listener also constructs meanings from and within the service in accordance with the structuring patterns characteristic of her or his stage of selfhood and faith. These structuring patterns constitute basic elements in the person's hermeneutics—the procedures of knowing, valuing, experiencing, and reasoning by which personal meanings are constructed and appropriated. Building on the previous chapter's descriptions of stages of faith and selfhood, let us consider some of the typical patterns of interest and interpretation we can anticipate in congregations.

Intuitive-Projective and Impulsive Presence

The Intuitive-Projective and impulsive presence in congregations is most obvious among children of preschool age. They bring the community their curiosity, their energy, their imaginations, and their special quality of living liminally. By living liminally I mean that children in this stage move freely back and forth across boundaries that they only later will sort out as dividing the conscious and the unconscious, or fantasy and reality. They also bring their impulsiveness and their need for a relational environment with a set of stories and symbols that can provide experiences and templates for the ordering of their souls.

This is the first stage in which we can explicitly begin to plant the seeds of vocation and partnership with God. By sharing biblical stories such as the calling of Moses and Samuel, of Joshua and the apostles, of Judith and Esther, and of Mary the mother of Christ, we can awaken a sense that our God is one who has special tasks in God's purposes for all who are willing to listen and respond. By providing relationships with older members of the community who have shaped vocation in accordance with offering their lives and work to God, we can begin to awaken them to membership in a *local* ethos of calling and response.

Our challenge in pastoral care with this stage is to provide for our children's forming faith and selfhood what Horace Bushnell called gifts to the imagination. We must share biblical narrative with our children in ways that are open-ended and that avoid tying the intriguing suggestiveness of story and parable too quickly to a moral or to moralistic meanings. As Jerome Berryman once put it, both we and they will be refreshed and informed by sharing biblical narratives in a way in which we "wonder together" about their meanings and implications.[3]

We are in the very early stages of understanding what the long-term impacts will be of the exposure of very young children to heavy doses of commercial television. We know that an important part of the work of the Intuitive-Projective stage is the forming of deep-going images that can hold together in a rudimentary coherence the child's experiences of everyday life. The symbols and stories of faith, mediated by personal relations of trustworthy affection, can enable him or her to incorporate into the early coherence of faith the threatening mysteries of death, evil impulses, power, and the uncanny. All of these are vividly alive to the child.[4] In the absence of an environment that mediates this kind of coherence with trustworthy affection, children are exposed to a vast hodgepodge of narrative and vivid sensation which exploits, without ordering, their fascination with violence, action, impulsive destructiveness, and death.[5]

Intuitive-Projective children are fascinated by the metaphysics of a God introduced to them as invisible and living in an inaccessible realm, and who is at the same time everywhere as a loving God.[6] Their fascination increases as they come to see this same God as one who entered our world as a helpless baby in a stable, taught, healed, loved, and preached the kingdom of God, and then died and was raised from the dead. Care requires that we listen carefully to what they do with these stories in their own constructions. We must listen for the distortions that mirror a chaotic and abusive relational environment in which a child may be caught. We must listen for the overconstricting appropriations children may make of the moralisms they have pressed upon them in church, at home, or by their peers. We must support one-parent households in providing consistent relational access to a parent substitute of the same sex at those critical times in early childhood when children are at risk of overinclusion with the parent of the opposite sex.[7] And we must find ways to reduce the dependence upon the mixed bag of commercial television as a prime mediator of images of the world and reality and as a substitute for relations with loving others and for the stories of faith. Our concerns in this regard carry us beyond the congregation. They press us toward that aspect of partnership with the creative work of God in which we share responsibility for the nurture toward wholeness of the children of our common entrustment.

Before we leave this stage and its congregational presence we should note that occasionally adolescents and adults exhibit the structural features of this stage. Typically when the liminality and emotional lability characteristic of this stage are encountered in adolescents or adults, we are dealing with episodes of regression or psychotic breakdown. There are, however, at the most primitive end of the fundamentalist spectrum some kinds of congregations which seem regularly to involve persons in collective manifestations of something very like the structurings of this stage. I have in mind cults that practice extreme forms of serpent handling and the ritual drinking of acid or poisons as tests and proofs of the magical, protective powers of the Spirit in behalf of the faithful. Such groups seem to provide religious sanction for the acting out of fantasies and impulses relating to violence, power, death, and miracle which show the primitive structures of unrestrained and unprotected early childhood.

Mythic-Literal and Imperial Presence

The presence in congregations of the Mythic-Literal stage of faith and the imperial stage of selfhood has some unique features. When the congregational context is one of middle- and upper-class parishes in the mainline Protestant or Catholic stream, this presence consists mainly of children of elementary and middle-school age. Some adolescents in these settings will also be best described by this stage, as will a limited number of adults. In other social-class settings, however, Mythic-Literal faith and imperial selfhood can constitute the modal developmental level for the community. Here again I have in mind certain fundamentalist and some Pentecostal communities. Though the structural features of faith and selfhood at this stage are similar in these two different kinds of settings, it makes a considerable difference whether this stage is experienced in a community as a way station on a longer journey or as having the characteristics of a final destination.

In both its childhood and adult forms this stage enables persons to construct a stable, linear, and predictable experience of the world. Cause-and-effect relations are understood; systems of classification and sorting have been created; simple perspective taking is a reliable acquisition. As I stressed in the last chapter, narrative emerges as the powerful and favored way of forming and conserving meanings and experience. This stage, however, is largely limited to the world of concrete experience and of literal interpretations of symbols and events. It does not yet rise to the level of reflective consideration of its stories and experiences in order to formulate meanings at a more generalized level.

From the standpoint of pastoral care one of the most valuable insights developmental theories offer us about this stage is its relatively undeveloped understanding of the interiority of persons—its own, and that of others. Almost in the manner of behaviorist psychology, persons of this stage have a view of others—and themselves (though without ever raising the question)—as being rather like Skinner's view of the psyche as a "black box." By this term he suggested that the structure of persons' interpretations, motivations, internal evaluations, and shaping of actions are largely inaccessible to scientific investigation and understanding. Moreover, he suggested that there may be little or no reliable relation between what people say they are going to do, the motives they claim, and what they actually do. Like Skinner, though without developing a theory of their position, persons best described by this stage are largely inattentive to the internal patterns that constitute their own and others' "personality."

In the absence of an ability to understand interiority, persons of this stage must construct some basis for discerning predictability and pattern in the behavior of God and other persons. Consistently we find that lawfulness and order are imposed on the universe in this stage by recourse to the idea of moral reciprocity. In simple fairness the cosmos is construed as rewarding good actions and as punishing bad actions. God is seen on the analogy of a stern but just and fair parent or ruler. In effect, this is a strong and clear narrative imposition of meaning based on a concrete understanding of cause-and-effect relations.

In young people this construction frequently gives way during a phase we have come to call eleven-year-old atheism. This phase comes when thoughtful children whose religious and social environments have given them sufficient emotional space to question and reckon for themselves begin to come to terms with the fact that ours is not a "quick-payoff universe." The good do not always get rewarded; the wicked are not always punished.

For other youths, however, where religious norms and beliefs have been enforced with rigidity and forms of emotional coercion, this construct of moral reciprocity becomes a more permanent fixture in their souls. Though they too may reject the God of the quick-payoff universe at the level of cognitive self-understanding, emotionally they get stuck in the structures of the Mythic-Literal stage. They move on into adolescent and eventually adult roles and relationships without the emotional freedom and the capacity for intimacy that are required for mutual interpersonal perspective taking. Often they operate in the areas of relations and religion with the kind of naive manipulation which first arose as a result of the embeddedness of the Mythic-Literal stage in the structure of its own interests, needs, and wishes. In fact, we see a fair number of persons—usually men—who may exhibit considerable cognitive sophistication in their occupational worlds (as physicians or engineers, for example) but who in their emotional and faith lives are rather rigidly embedded in the structures of Mythic-Literal faith and imperial selfhood. To their marriages and family life they bring a rigidity—often coupled with authoritarian patterns—that inflicts psychic and sometimes physical violence on their partners and children. It often leads them to a kind of baffled bereftness in their forties and fifties, when in the shambles of their shattered families, for the first time they may begin the painful task of learning about the interior lives of selves—starting with their own.

Whether at thirteen, when it comes much more naturally and pain-

lessly, or at fifty-three, when it comes out of the agony of broken relationships, the movement into mutual interpersonal perspective taking opens
the way for a reflective relation to the self and others which gives one access
to the world of the self's interiority. It seems clear to me after a number of
years of observation that we cannot be more intimate with others than we
are ready to be with ourselves. Similarly, we cannot be more intimate with
God than we are prepared to be with ourselves and others. The emergence
of mutual interpersonal perspective taking prepares the way for a new
structure of faith and selfhood whenever it appears.

Synthetic-Conventional and Interpersonal Presence

A large number of persons in the congregation, if it is typical, will be
best described by the Synthetic-Conventional stage of faith and the interpersonal stage of selfhood. With varying degrees of intensity they bring to
the service the desire to be in a relationship with God and with the important persons of their lives in which they feel that they are living up to the
expectations these important others have of them. Prayers of confession
and penance will be construed as occasions for asking forgiveness for failures of attitude and action and for restoration in the love and acceptance of
God. Persons best described by these stages feel that their very selfhood is
constituted by their roles and their relationships. It is likely, therefore, that
any sense of alienation from God they experience will be derived from or
closely related to feelings of estrangement or tension with persons from
their circle of family, lovers, friends, work associates, and acquaintances.
When the sermon or prayers of petition include concern for the welfare of
persons from other social classes or other nations, this group will likely
envision both needs and solutions in interpersonal terms. From the sermon they hope for a sense of emotional confirmation of their personhood
and a sense of warmth and connectedness with the priest or pastor. They
hunger for a sense of confirmation in the meanings they invest in the roles
and relationships that constitute their selfhood. They may feel a special
gladness in thinking of the congregation as an intergenerational community bound together in friendship and shared experiences. Such persons
long for harmony and conflict-free interliving in the community of faith.
Conflict and controversy are disturbing to them because they seem to
threaten the basis of community. The maintenance of peace and the restoration of good feelings and unity within the community frequently loom

as far more important to them than dealing with issues that might cause conflict.

The underlying metaphor for the church most commonly held by persons described here is that of the ideal or romanticized extended family. The community of faith is seen as a network of persons related through their common values and beliefs in God and their common love for Jesus Christ. These values and beliefs do not need to be made too explicit; it is sensed that such an effort might lead to disagreements and breaches of relationships. The important thing is to provide mutual support in times of trouble or difficulty, and to maintain a supportive web of interpersonal connectedness through the community of faith.

The kind of persons we have been describing often constitute the most consistent corps of committed workers and servers in the church. Though they typically are not innovative leaders, they have a special sensitivity and fidelity to those parts of the gospel that call for bearing one another's burdens and for building up the body of Christ. They bring gifts of inclusion and care for each person in the community, and often their loyalty to the church, viewed as extended family, can sustain them in a kind of acceptance of and loyalty to others whose faith outlook may be somewhat threatening to their own. They have limited ability to take account of the systems that shape, constrain, and sometimes oppress persons. They have difficulty in relating their faith to social, economic, and political structures. Analytic approaches to religious experience and to the central symbols of the faith may be uninteresting or threatening to such persons. In confrontation with pastoral leadership or groups who insist upon critical and analytic approaches to matters of faith, persons of the Synthetic-Conventional and interpersonal stage may take a stance that seems anti-intellectual, oriented to emotions and experience, and defensively conventional.

In pastoral counseling with persons in this stage there are a number of predictable sources of struggle and dis-ease that derive from the structuring of Synthetic-Conventional faith and interpersonal selfhood. Because of the absence of third-person perspective taking, persons in this stage are overdependent upon significant others and the community for confirmation in selfhood and faith. Adults in this stage have internalized significant others from previous years who help to play a balancing and guiding role in their internal life. And there is a collection of present face-to-face relations that are significant. It is likely for church-oriented adults in this stage that the pastor and some other persons who have institutionally important roles in their lives, such as bosses, respected associates, and community leaders, are invested with a kind of double significance or weight as regards the maintenance of a sense of selfhood and self-esteem. Crises or times of distress can arise when a person feels dissonance between himself or herself and one or more of these significant others. Dissonance can also occur when two or more of the important authorities in one's life are in conflict or serious disagreement. Similarly, experiences of conflicting role expectations can be upsetting and disorienting.

In all these cases the person feels distress which he or she cannot resolve because there is no transcending standpoint from which the issues leading to tensions, struggles, or conflicts can be seen, evaluated, and adjudicated. The role of counseling and pastoral support in these instances calls initially for providing a vicarious experience of third-person perspective taking and inviting the person to view and evaluate things from that standpoint. Developmentally helpful counseling calls for a kind of teaching and modeling which can help persons in this stage recognize the possibility of a third-person perspective—its liberation and responsibility—and to provide support in beginning to rely upon it and exercise the new quality of self-authorization it brings. In this pastoral alliance several kinds of resistance can be expected. Throughout there will likely be a dynamic arising from the person's recognition of dependence upon the pastor and other authorities which gives rise to feelings of gratitude and affection, on the one hand, but also to often unrecognized feelings of resentment, on the other. The resentment, coupled with anxieties about change, about one's ability to cope with new responsibilities, and about the effects of new self-authorization on one's network of relations, can make the person ambivalent about the course of pastoral counseling.

From a different source, persons in this stage are likely to experience a special kind of crisis at times of loss or threat to their central relationships and roles. Since identity and faith are inextricably tied up with these central roles and relationships, events such as the death of a spouse or close friend, divorce, retirement, or sudden unemployment can have devastating effects. The grief or loss takes on a special power because the role or relation (or both) that has been lost constituted one of the fundamental elements of one's sense of self. The loss drastically diminishes the sense of selfhood and threatens its very existence. At such times the person, deeply at risk, needs a consistent and continuing outpouring of community assurance about the worth, the value, the identity, and the special selfhood that the person continues to have in the eyes of those who care for him or her. Developmentally it becomes a time to face the question, Who am I when I am not defined by this key relation or role which has been taken from me? It can be a time of deepening one's reliance and relation for selfhood and faith upon God and the community. It can also be a time for claiming a different kind of basis for one's faith and sense of self. In either case one needs consistent affirmation and support in reconstructing the bases of one's selfhood and outlook.

Individuative-Reflective and Institutional Presence

In many congregations another substantial presence is constituted by that group of persons who may best be described by the Individuative-Reflective stage of faith and the institutional stage of selfhood. In the fully developed forms of this stage, persons come to worship aware of an "I" or a sense of selfhood that has emerged to control and manage the various roles and relations that make up their life structures. This "I" has had to struggle to some significant degree with those external authorities—both personal and institutional—that guide, constrain, and support one in growth toward adulthood. It also has dealt in some clear ways with the internalized voices of parents and other authorities from the past. From the service of worship, the prayers, and the preaching, the person of this stage wants an acknowledgment of and support in her or his self-authorization. Worship needs to recognize and celebrate the hard-won assumption of responsibility for choices regarding life style and beliefs. This stage wants what it perceives to be a fully adult form of worship and faith.

At the same time, however, persons in this stage seem to ask the church to provide, in worship and community, spaces and relationships in which the stress of consciously orchestrating and managing the self-responsible self can periodically be relaxed. Persons who perceive themselves to be rowing their own boats in competitive, multiformly demanding circumstances respond to communities of others like themselves where it is safe to let down a bit. They find release in acknowledging their need for relationship and solidarity with like-minded others. Worship and other settings will make this possible if they combine a certain measure of intellectual stimulation and challenge with a quality of community fellowship that does not try to reimpose external and conventional religious expectations and authority.

The underlying metaphor for church correlated with this stage is likely to be a kind of unspoken pragmatic, contractual individualism. One *has* roles, relationships, commitments, and intentions. One *has* a now more explicit and clear set of beliefs and values. Church is valued and Christian faith is interpreted in accordance with the contribution it makes to supporting and extending the perspectives and commitments that express and support one's selfhood. Depending on the depth and intensity of one's commitments, Christian faith can also constitute a source of accountability and normative direction for one's selfhood and goals. The Christian tradition can be selectively appropriated and interpreted to shape and support one's individuative orientation. In this process, demythologization and conceptual restatements of central elements and symbols of the tradition are welcomed and relied upon.

Persons best described by the stage of Individuative-Reflective faith and institutional selfhood have an often unrecognized need for both a confessional and a wailing wall. The structuring patterns of this stage and the pressures of our particular culture place heavy burdens on persons of Individuative faith to be tubs that sit on their own bottoms. These persons are called to be self-sufficient, self-starting, self-managing, and self-repairing units. In the absence of a trusted community of others with whom one shares central meanings and values and with whom one can afford to disclose the self in depth, this set of expectations can lead to privatized and sick self-dialogues. When things are going well, persons caught in this privatization are vulnerable to forms of inflation and inflated self-deception. They may identify with self-aggrandizing personal images that result from the continual pressure to overadvertise the self and to identify with the advertisements. In that state of overinflation they can fall into the trap of allowing themselves privileges and moral leeway that later prove to be terribly destructive of work patterns and of relationships and values which they temporarily took for granted. On the other hand, the person who is too dependent upon private self-dialogue for the maintenance of a sense of self and direction is also subject to deflation and excessive despair about the self when things go badly. The pervasive individualism that characterizes this society—and too often our churches as well—makes difficult the provision of a context of pastoral care to persons caught in these dangerous orientations. It is imperative that we develop groups where persons who are susceptible to the pressures I have described can find trustworthy community with peers. We need to provide circles where the armor of their defenses can be ventilated and where they can stand to submit their images of self to one another—and to the gospel—for correction.

The Individuative-Reflective orientation responds to, and often demands, a different quality of religious leadership from the Synthetic-Conventional stage. It is impatient with "mystery-mastery" approaches to religious leadership, in which leaders attempt to heighten and perpetuate dependence upon them by accentuating awareness of their special training, their ordination, and the complexity and mystery of the matters of faith. Individuative-Reflective types welcome being made partners in inquiry into the sources of faith. They enjoy going "into the kitchen" with the preacher or pastor to join in the struggle of making sense of particular texts or elements in the tradition. They have a preference for a reasoned and reasoning faith. They tend to fear obscurantism more than they fear admitting that faith may not provide all the necessary answers to ethical and religious questions. They have the capability—and often the interest—to engage in inquiry into the tradition to find new resources for the effort to relate faith to their lives and challenges in the world.[8]

Commonly those churches which have as their modal developmental level the Synthetic-Conventional and interpersonal stage have found it hard to make space and welcome for the Individuative types. By the same token, persons in transition to or already equilibrated in the Individuative stage often find life in Synthetic-Conventional communities stifling and dull. Clashes or antipathies between persons in these two stages represent one common form of "cross-stage static." Enabling such groups to coexist and work together with integrity in a church represents, when it occurs, one of the major accomplishments of pastoral leadership and care.

Conjunctive and Inter-Individual Presence

Generally persons best described by the Conjunctive and inter-individual stage have reckoned with the paradox that God's self-revelation is always a matter of both disclosure and concealment. They have come to know in their bone marrow that the mystery we name God can only partially be represented in our best symbols and parables. They bring to church a tensive conviction that "it is meet, right, and our bounden duty" to pray, praise, and proclaim the reality and love of God. At the same time, they instinctively avoid the kind of symbolic domestication that makes favored formulations and doctrines into idolatrous and shoddy graven images of an exceedingly elusive transcendent reality. I am trying to describe a dialectical form of faith and selfhood in which persons find it necessary to affirm perspectives that maintain polar tensions in faith. God is both transcendent and immanent; God cannot be contained in anthropocentric categories, yet there is that which is personal in our experience and testimony to God.

Most of the persons who can be identified with this stage are at midlife or beyond. Occasionally, by virtue of early experiences of suffering and loss, or because of a kind of precocious spiritual or religious seriousness, a younger person may move into the Conjunctive stage. But usually, like that brokerage firm that advertises that it "makes money the old-fashioned way," such persons *earn* it. They earn it by having taken on irrevocable responsibilities for others or for some sector of our shared life. They earn it by having their noses rubbed in our finitude, through the sacrament of failure and through the death or loss of loved ones. They earn it by recognizing that our feelings of autonomy and self-control as a species, and our vaunted capacities for the technical management of our vastly interdependent systems, are maintained at the price of considerable self-deception and illusion. Put positively, they have come to the conviction that the principal acting units in human and divine history are the great social and economic systems of which we are a part. Individual human beings, while responsible and gifted with a measure of genuine freedom, must learn to exert that freedom effectively in the interdependence of systems.

Selfhood at this stage no longer focuses its concern so heavily on control and self-management and on maintaining the boundaries of a consciously chosen set of affiliations and commitments. In this stage, concern with selfhood becomes a matter of attending to deeper movements of the spirit within and of working at disciplines by which to discern and integrate elements from the unconscious structuring and wisdom of the self into consciousness. The self continues to be a responsible actor and agent in her or his world. In that action and agency, however, the agenda is set less by socially determined aspirations and more by attention to the subtle but insistent impulsions of the spirit.

In this attending to the impulsions of spirit, the person of Conjunctive faith and inter-individual selfhood should not be understood primarily in Jungian terms. There the guiding truths and insights for one's individuation are seen as coming from one's psyche, with its archetypes and symbols and its balancing responsiveness to the ordering and integrative power of the collective unconscious. In contrast, the Christian of this stage is learning to trust the Christian tradition in new ways and at new depth. Its symbols, doctrines, narratives, and rituals are acknowledged as structuring means of grace. Prayer and discernment become modes of opening oneself and attending radically—that is, with both conscious attention and a responsiveness of the deeper self—to the truth that takes form and comes to expression in the Scriptures and tradition and in the living interpretations of the community of faith.

In Conjunctive faith and in communities influenced by it, there is a taste for the stranger. Persons have begun to learn to acknowledge and live with their strangers within—their own spirit and unconscious life. Having an experience of the disclosure and concealment of God in revelatory traditions, they begin to encounter the religious traditions of others as strangers that may be sources of new depth of insight and of correction in our appropriation of our own traditions. Further, for Christians there seems to be in this stage a coming to terms, at stirring new depths, with both Jesus Christ as the liberating and redeeming stranger and with the Christ's radical sense of solidarity with the despised or oppressed stranger.

There is an affinity between the structuring of the Conjunctive stage and the understanding of church which we described in chapter 1 as the public church. While an approach to the public church can be taught and formed appropriately with Christians of each of the stages, it or something very like it is essential to the integrity of persons of the Conjunctive stage. Such persons have the capacity to understand and relate to Christians of each of the other stages. In this sense, they can serve as sponsors and guarantors for others. At the same time, from the depth of their Christian commitments they have a capacity to receive, and to dialogue at depth with, the faith witnesses of people from other traditions.

But there are pitfalls for Conjunctive Christians, as well. In ways that are perhaps distinctive to this stage, people can feel a deep sense of cosmic aloneness or homelessness. The dark side of their awareness of God's revelation, both as disclosure and concealment, lies in a deepened appreciation of the otherness and the nonavailability of God. The dark side of their receptiveness to the witness and truth of other traditions can be a subdued sense of the imperative to share and commend the Christian story in evangelization. The dark side of their awareness of our being enmeshed in vast and complex systems can be a sense of paralysis and a retreat into a private world of spirituality. Having had their eyes burned by all that they see and have seen, Conjunctive Christians can fall into a kind of immobility that—if prolonged—cuts the nerve of the call to partnership with God. In these respects Christians best described by the Conjunctive stage need—as do Christians of the other stages—the gifts and the structuring orientations of persons of other stages to encounter them with correcting emphases and energies.

CO-PRESENCE AND ONGOING CONVERSION IN THE CONGREGATION

To the author it is all too clear that this chapter could be extended into a substantial book. Its subject matter deserves a much more extended treatment. In the present context, however, it may be helpful to draw together several concluding observations with regard to certain questions with which we began.

The characterizations of developmental styles of congregational presence are meant to help give flesh and blood to the descriptions of stages of faith and selfhood provided in chapter 4. In the preamble to this chapter I emphasized the importance of avoiding irresponsible categorizing of persons and groups with these stages. I acknowledged the normative character of the stage theories of faith and selfhood and affirmed that steady support and encouragement should be given to keep development, as a byproduct of faithfulness in vocation, in process. I also cautioned against making development an end in itself or seeing movement from one stage to another as something that can be accelerated or pushed. We must always remember that genuine development in faith and selfhood, and the ongoing *metanoia* of real conversions, are the results of both our work and encouragement *and* the empowerment of the Holy Spirit.

It should be clearer now that stages of selfhood and faith describe fairly broad and comprehensive patterns in persons' ways of construing self and world in relation to God, and in the deep emotions and dispositions that form around those ways. Moreover, I hope it is becoming clear that our comprehensive constructions and emotional dispositions in faith and selfhood involve networks that include communities of others and the historical and institutional frameworks of those communities. Ronald Marstin's book *Beyond Our Tribal Gods*[9] is of crucial importance for understanding these matters. Marstin, with a strong grounding in sociological theory, helps us see how transition from one stage to another, especially in adulthood, involves moving from one community of primary belonging to another. He does not mean that literally we must leave our particular parish or denomination—though it could come to that. Rather, his point is that in the deconstruction and reconstruction of our ways of being in faith that the transition between stages requires, we literally disembed ourselves from our previous worlds of relation, discourse, and belonging. We then have to struggle to bring the new structuring of faith and selfhood taking form in us into integral relations with a new community of interpretation and commitment. Transition from one stage to another in childhood and adolescence can have its rough spots and struggles, to be sure, but typically the gradual reconstruction and elaboration of structures of knowing and valuing involved in early transitions between stages are not too difficult. But for reasons Marstin's work helps us see, things can become more difficult, protracted, and even dangerous with stage transitions in adulthood. Let us look for a moment at what I have elsewhere called the "optimal" correlations between stages of faith and selfhood and what we might call psychosocial "seasons" of our lives:[10]

Infancy	Primal faith, incorporative self
Preschool age	Intuitive-Projective faith, impulsive self
Midchildhood	Mythic-Literal faith, imperial self
Adolescence	Synthetic-Conventional faith, interpersonal self
Young adulthood	Individuative-Reflective faith, institutional self
Middle adulthood	Conjunctive faith, inter-individual self
Middle adulthood and beyond	Universalizing faith, God-grounded self

When I speak of optimal correlations of life season and faith stage I am referring to what appear to me to be a kind of "natural" fit between the psychosocial and physical processes of development and the structuring qualities underlying the correlated stages of selfhood and faith. As our previous discussions have made clear, however, one can encounter biological and functional adults who are best described by any of the stages from the Intuitive-Projective and impulsive stage on. Implicitly I have wanted to communicate that if one equilibrates or "locks in" at one of the two childhood stages and carries that stage on through the season of adolescence and into adulthood, it gets more and more difficult to undertake transition to the next stage.[11] Similarly, if a young adult carries the Synthetic-Conventional stage well beyond her twenties and early thirties, the probability grows that she will face difficulties in making the eventual transition to the Individuative-Reflective stage and beyond.

Correlations between stages of faith and selfhood and life seasons are made more complex by what, following Kenneth Kenniston,[12] I have spoken of as the modal developmental level in faith and selfhood which we find in congregations, denominations, and perhaps in businesses and informal social and friendship groupings. The modal developmental level, as I stated earlier, is the average expectable level of development for adults in a given community—of faith or otherwise. If an adult does not develop to the modal level, he or she is made to feel deviant and somewhat deficient. If, on the other hand, a person develops to a stage beyond the mode, then he or she is also made to feel deviant. There is a powerful if subtle coerciveness about the modal developmental level in a community.

What I am about to propose now is not based on empirical social-scientific research. It comes, rather, from theoretical reflection and practical experience in congregations of many sorts. I believe that the distinctive challenge and calling of what in chapter 1 I called the public church is that it does and should pioneer in the creation and development of "multimodal" communities of faith. By this I mean that the public church, whether large or small, urban, suburban, or rural, should make allowance for the variety of stages of faith and selfhood in its congregation, from infancy to maturity. It should work consciously and intentionally to become a nurturing and stimulating ecology of care and vocation, meeting and embracing persons at their various points of development. In order to do this, however, it must have a stage level of aspiration which guides and informs its patterns of pastoral care, its lay and pastoral leadership, and its work in education. The stage level of aspiration for a public church, it seems clear, is Conjunctive faith.

I stand by my warning that faith development, understood as movement from one stage to another, should not be the primary goal of pastoral care and pastoral leadership. That kind of development comes as a byproduct of our work and that of the spirit of God as we try to be faithfully responsive to the call of God to partnership. As a practical level of aspiration, however, the Conjunctive stage provides an informing way of appropriating and entering into the Christian memory and hope. With regard and care for persons at each of the earlier stages, it nonetheless keeps our preaching, teaching, and pastoral care open-ended toward continuing growth in relation to the call of God. In this sense the Conjunctive stage as a level of aspiration and the Universalizing stage—which keeps the Conjunctive stage itself open-ended—constitute part of the eschatological pressure of God's coming kingdom. The tension between aspiration and acceptance which this approach envisions aims to be faithful to the divine call to ongoing *metanoia*—ongoing repentance and conversion—toward God's goal of a universal commonwealth of love and justice.

This perspective envisions congregations that will organize themselves and their pastoral care as ecologies supportive of multiple modal levels of faith and selfhood. At the same time, it envisions leading persons in ongoing growth in faithful responsiveness to the call of God to partnership. This means, of course, caring for persons in transition and in the ongoing *metanoia* of development in faith and selfhood. Care for persons in times of transition and transformation requires that we look next at change as an explicit focus of pastoral attention and concern.

CHAPTER 6

Faith and the
Dynamics
of Change

If there is anything we can safely assume that we share with all of our contemporaries in a society like ours, it is the experience of relentless, ongoing, disruptive, and dislocating change. Echoing Saint Paul we can say that we have been changed, we are being changed, we will be changed. Margaret Mead, who was born at the beginning of the twentieth century and died in 1975, claimed—rightly, I believe—that her generation had dealt with more massive, protracted, and accelerating change than any prior generation in recorded history. Sixteen years ago Alvin Toffler speculated in his book *Future Shock* that perhaps we modern human beings were reaching the limits of our capacities for constructive adaptation to rapid, multilayered change.

Astrophysicist J. McKim Malville proposes to us, on the basis of twentieth-century quantum physics and relativity theory, that change is literally the law and necessity of our expanding universe:

> Guided by recent discoveries in the new physical sciences we have moved into a new reality in the twentieth century which can only be described as opulent. At the heart of that opulence lies unrelenting change. Many of the old immutabilities of the universe have been dissolved in the fires of quantum mechanics, relativity, and cosmology, and have been replaced by a microcosm which changes in rhythm with the changing macrocosm. . . .
> Change penetrates so deeply into the matter and energy of the universe that the ultimate meaning of our lives may be perceived in the promise of perpetual newness. Yet, how rarely do we appreciate our world's extraordinary and so very necessary vitality. For instance, the most fundamental quality of our universe is the continuing expansion of space and the consequent departure of its contents from equilibrium and stability. Were the universe not expanding we would not be around to ask cosmic questions or to be amazed and puzzled. Were the universe not out of equilibrium, the improba-

bles like you and like me, the giraffe and the rhinoceros would certainly not be present. Only a dull, warm broth of matter and energy would inhabit the universe.[1]

In the journey of this book the treatment of change has been largely implicit rather than explicit. In considering the work of practical theology in chapter 1 we approached it as an ongoing, alternating process of action and reflection. Practical theology, we suggested, arises out of issues that emerge as the community of faith seeks to be faithful to its mission in the midst of changing situations and challenges. Focusing on *praxis,* practical theology is dynamic in its use of categories and in its responsiveness to changing circumstances. Then when we looked at vocation and covenant community in chapter 2, I proposed that we see vocation as a dynamic relation of partnership with God and others whom God has called. Vocation implies a relationship in which we engage in ongoing times of negotiation with God and the covenant community, in order to discern and keep accountable in our callings. Chapter 3 sought to show the dynamism of God's action in the universe and in our history, and to propose an elaboration of metaphors by which we can see and align ourselves with the working of God. In its use of both process and historicist approaches, that chapter attempted to move beyond the static imagery of classical theism. Chapters 4 and 5, by their treatment of the stages of faith and selfhood that mark the path of a lifetime of ongoing growth and development, bespeak an effort to see human lives, in response to the ongoing action of God, as being in motion. In each of the chapters of the book, therefore, change has been assumed as fundamental. Motion at many levels has been an underlying assumption of the work. And yet at no point until now have we made change and transition the focal foreground rather than the background of our attention. Not until now have we sought to focus directly on the processes and dynamics of change. To do this is essential for our treatment of faith development and pastoral care.

SOURCES AND TYPES OF CHANGE
IN OUR LIVES

I want to suggest that we can fruitfully identify three broad categories of the sources and types of change with which we must deal. These categories are not watertight compartments. Any one of the types of sources of change is likely to interact with another. Change begun in one of these areas of our experience may well precipitate change in another. Yet I think that the distinctions between them may be helpful: (1) *Developmental change:* By this I point to change that results from the maturation and formation of the self. (2) *Reconstructive change:* Here I will discuss change as breakdown and rebuilding, restoration and healing, conversion and transformation. (3) *Change as response to intrusive marker events:* Intrusive marker events are those times in our lives when disruptive events happen to us that affect our lives pervasively. They alter the patterns of our lives fundamentally. A marker event is one after which in some significant sense one's life is never the same again.

Developmental Change

With developmental change, we have in view change as the process of construction and formation of the self. Development occurs, in our experience, as a complex pattern of alternation between times of equilibrium and disequilibrium. Robert Kegan, in teaching the thought of Jean Piaget about disequilibrium in developmental change, likes to point out that walking is a controlled fall. One moves nowhere on foot without coming unbalanced. Development is a process of alternations between times of provisional balance and coming unbalanced, then finding a recovered balance in a new place. The complexity of this pattern, however, comes from the fact that in the course of maturation and development there are many different dimensions, levels, and rates of development and change occurring in us simultaneously. We have names for some of these levels:

Biological or bodily maturation. Earlier we noted the foundational aspect of selfhood constituted by our bodies. In the course of bodily maturation, stabilization, and eventual decline, we undergo many predictable changes. Yet there are elements and factors that are unique to each of us. And further, our own experiences, even of predictable and shared steps in biological aging, are new to us when they come and are uniquely our own. With biological changes come alterations in our social roles and our self-image. Aging and the waxing and waning of our bodily energy and vitality are also events in our spiritual lives.

Perceptual and cognitive development. Built into our presentation of developmental stages of faith and selfhood was an accounting of the sequence of stagelike balances in the ways we perceive, construct, interpret, and make sense of our world of experience. In the tradition of Jean Piaget, we gave attention to a series of revolutions in the operations of knowing and understanding that are of fundamental importance for faith and selfhood. Changes in the structuring of our knowing and valuing lead to the reconstruction of our memories of the past and our anticipations of the future. They result in reworkings of our constructions of self-other, self-world relations, as well as of our compositions of ultimate reality.

Emotional and affective maturation. Here we speak about the formation of patterns of feeling and sentiment, of course. But much more is involved. We have in view the formation of our more long-lasting attitudes and values. Affective development includes the formation of the habitual dispositions and the deep longings and motives of our lives.

Capacities for moral and social responsibility. In our accounting of stages of faith and selfhood we gave special attention to the role of social perspective taking in the construing of experience and the interpretation of meanings. Capacities for perspective taking have a developmental history related to cognition and social experience. Those capacities, wed with gains in cognitive development, constitute the developmental foundations of moral reasoning and of conceptions of social justice and responsibility.

Development in faith. In a major sense, development in faith includes all the development strands we have described here. It traces development in the ability to grasp our lives as grounded in the reality of Being and in the ability to live out of that awareness in relation to our neighbors. As such, faith involves biological, cognitive, emotional, and moral-reasoning development. It marshals all these dimensions of the self in response to God's being and action as made discernible through those moments of God's self-disclosure which we call revelation.

An accounting of change brought about by development and maturation could, of course, go on almost endlessly. Change in our lives originating in these sectors has a certain predictability and periodicity. As Erik Erikson subtitled one of his early articles, we are dealing with the "growth and crises of the healthy personality." "Crisis," of course derives from the Greek *krisis,* which means simply "turning point"—the point where things must change. Crisis, it is well to remember, does not necessarily mean change for the worse or for negativity. The crisis point in a battle, a love relationship, an illness, or a political campaign means, rather, the point where things must change. The coin must drop, one way or the other. When the word "crisis" was first translated into Chinese, the translators insightfully used the two Chinese characters meaning "danger" and "opportunity."

Developmental transitions can be long and protracted. Any change that affects us across the range of developmental strands we have considered here involves us in a pretty comprehensive regrounding of our sense of self, our ways of relating to others, and our ways of construing the basic conditions of our existence. Developmental transitions may also bring the need to develop new skills, attitudes, or beliefs, or to find new symbols and stories to guide us in our action or response.

Developmental theories of many kinds, including theories of selfhood and faith, have emerged to help us map these processes of psychosocial, emotional, cognitive, and moral development. Taken separately and together they begin to illumine the patterns of a general set of "ground plans" or "blueprints" that make visible the contours and directions of our genetic potentiation for covenant partnership with God and with each other. Developmental theories promise to help practical theology in its effort to clarify the path by which we become subjects in relation to God.

Reconstructive Change

With reconstructive change, I have in view personal change as including transformation and reconstruction, breakdown and rebuilding, restoration and healing, or conversion and the redirection of life. Few of us ever make fundamental changes in the shape of our character or in the deep patterns of our personalities by elective choice alone. The need or imperative for deep-going change in our lives usually comes in response to some experience of shipwreck, of failure in love or work, or of spiritual struggle or illumination. In a later section we will deal with times of radical change that are due to intrusive events in our lives. Though there is inevitably some overlap between these two categories, here I want to focus on reconstructive work in our lives made necessary by the legacy of wounds, warps, or fallibilities which became part of our selfhood in the processes of our growth and development. Included among these flawed and weakened areas of our souls are those which grow out of the choices and influences that others and our environments imposed upon us. Also included are the deficiencies resulting from our own choices, neglects, and persistent weaknesses. In trying to find a language to talk about these sources of dis-ease in our lives and the lives of others, we are very close to the boundary line

where psychological and theological accounts of human weakness, vulner
ability, and failure intersect. We are speaking of those aspects of finitude
which have traditionally been called the "tinder of sin"—the stuff in our
lives where sin finds ignitable materials. We are trying to point to the
personal contents of the Fall in our lives. We are trying to speak of these
matters in a way that does justice to the strange mixture of befallenness
(that which happens to us beyond our ability to influence it) and fallenness
(that which happens to us and shapes our ways of being selves in which we
have to acknowledge some degree of complicity, awareness, and assent).
What makes times of breakdown, failure, and deconstruction so important in our lives is that they, with all the pain they bring, represent occasions when some significant structure of our befallen-fallenness has to be
addressed.

None of us moves through the process of ongoing development without
accumulating scar tissue, injured joints, crippled emotions, and distorted
patterns of relating to others. None of us escapes, either, the consequences
of wrong choices others made for us, or wrong choices we have made for
ourselves—with whatever degree of consciousness and capacity for choice
we had at those points in our lives. To some degree Carson McCullers's
statement in *The Ballad of the Sad Cafe* fits all of us: "Only the wounded,"
she says, "can serve in the army of the Lord." This means, of course, that
all of us are candidates.

There are varying degrees of woundedness, however. There are varying
degrees of deprivation, lack, and distortion. Befallenness is not equally
distributed in this world, and some persons have a lot more leeway for
fallenness than others. Our traditional theological doctrines of sin have
not served us adequately regarding these subtleties. For now it is enough
to say that all of us have and probably can recognize fairly significant
dimensions of our ways of being persons that could accurately be called
neurotic. I refer to these as "squishy" places in our psychic structures—
places that give rise to departures from the sort of balance, evenhanded-
ness, and capacities for undistorted relations that mark our utopias of
personhood. These are our blind spots or our blind sides; they are the
sources of our myopia and defensiveness; they are our spongy areas of
vulnerability and weakness.

We reserve the term "neurotic" to describe those troublesome aspects
of our personalities in which we are vulnerable to the kind of distortions of
behavior and communication that fall within the range considered normal. To varying degrees we all are subject to deeper and more dangerous

distortions as well. In ways we usually have little awareness of until forced to delve into them, many of us carry in our souls the consequences of painful early experiences: emotional or actual abandonments, psychic or physical violence and abuse, or parents who loved us too smotheringly or devouringly. We may carry deep wounds from the ambiguous love of incestuous fathers or brothers or from neighbors or big sisters who exploited our sex. There may be deep rage smoldering explosively from having always come in second—or third or fourth. One may carry a nebulous resentment and sense of stagnation rooted in the personality's control by a too effectively installed superego. One may conform excessively to the expectations of authorities, owing to a structure of guilt that resulted from the infant death of a younger sibling whom one had heartily despised. One can have a self-destructive anger expressed in contempt for oneself, and for others of one's kind, because of the overt and oppressive prejudices of a favored racial majority—and on and on and on.

With whatever degree and sources of fallenness and befallenness that mark our lives, sooner or later many of us come to times when the stories we are living get stuck. It may be that we reach a certain period in our lives when we seem to have lost our energy, purpose, or sense of direction. Maybe we have buried ourselves under loads of responsibilities and obligations undertaken to prove ourselves once and for all, or to get someone's attention and approval. Perhaps under the pressure of a developmental transition, or in the context of a buildup of institutional or familial pressures, or in the crisis precipitated by an extramarital affair, some significant sector of the structure of ongoing life collapses or threatens to collapse. At such times we find ourselves in need of space and help to do deconstructive and reconstructive work in our lives.

Change as Response to Intrusive Marker Events

Imagine a contemporary seminar or workshop on change resulting from intrusive marker events. Who might be in attendance? Though it is by no means an exhaustive list, such a seminar could include any of the following:

- several men or women recently separated or divorced
- some couples who are newly wed or newly re-wed
- a man in his twenties or thirties who has suddenly acquired a ready-made family of four children
- a single parent who has recently adopted his or her first child

- several widows and widowers
- one or more newly retired persons
- a few persons who at or near midlife are changing careers or reentering careers after several years out
- one who is recovering from a first heart attack; another who has a cancer in remission
- one or more political refugees from El Salvador
- a physician and spouse emigrating from South Africa
- a pregnant teenager, along with another in the aftermath of an abortion
- one or more who have recently become unemployed
- a couple whose son or daughter has just shared with them that he or she is gay
- a man or woman who has recently received a major promotion and raise
- an older adult who has recently lost a grown son or daughter to a brief illness or an accident
- a recent winner of a multimillion state-lottery prize
- a young marine just back from six months of firing and being fired upon in Beirut

The list could go on. As we said earlier, marker events in our lives are events after which our lives are never the same again. Some marker events are of course less disruptive than others. Some of them come more or less on schedule as part of the expectable flow of our lives. These events, such as graduations, leaving home, marriage, the birth of children, certain kinds of successes and achievements, our children's marriages, their home leavings, our retirements, etc., can be anticipated and rehearsed to some degree. Many of these are happy events; we do not expect them to be upsetting. And yet when they come we often find that the adjustments they require and the emotions they arouse are greater and more disruptive than we had anticipated.

And then there are marker events that blast the landscape of our lives and shred the veil of our temples beyond all recognition. These devastating events, against which none of us finally has protection or guarantees, can be prepared for—in limited ways—only by shaping a life grounded in faith and a community of faith that can form and support us in spiritual communication with a Ground of Being beyond our finite bonds of love and our webs of woven meanings.

In this part of our book we have focused on sources and types of change in our lives. For the most part we have been concerned with personal rather than social or systemic change. Now we must ask whether there may be some underlying rhythm or process in our experience of undergoing change in all three of the categories I have identified. Is there, underlying and linking together the experience of change from each of these sources, a fundamental process of response and reintegration whose structure and flow we can identify? I believe so. Let us turn now to a consideration of such a ground rhythm of change with an eye to assessing its helpfulness for our interest in faith development and pastoral care and for strengthening the congregation as an ecoiogy of care and vocation.

DYNAMICS OF CHANGE

To speak of the dynamics of change may give one the feeling of trying to roller-skate on a lazy Susan. We usually associate a dynamic with something volatile and changing. But the Greek root of the word "dynamic"—*dynamis*—literally means "power." In its usual association with spirit, it connotes directional power, or power directed and structured purposefully. Therefore, to speak of the dynamics of change is to invite our attention to change as structured process and as powerful and transformative process.

A number of authors have written helpfully about the patterns and rhythms of change in our lives, and about how communities and care givers can minister to persons involved in deep-going change.[2] I want to highlight a few gleanings from the work of William Bridges.[3] Bridges sees the dynamics of important change in our lives as involving three major phases: endings, the neutral zone, and new beginnings.

Endings

What we call the beginning is often the end
And to make an end is to make a beginning
The end is where we start from.
—T. S. Eliot, "Little Gidding"

Each significant ending in our life involves to some degree a symbolic death. Teachers know this. I have a good friend whose vocation centers in empowering fifth graders to relish using the written word with skill and freedom, to capture and communicate their meanings. She has learned that both she and her children need about six weeks to say goodbye. Early in her teaching career she noted that in the last week or so of school the children turned uncharacteristically cranky. They found fault with class-room procedures that had previously made for order and joy. They griped at the teacher and resented her directions. A kind of sullenness seeped into their writings and general attitudes. Reflecting on this, my friend—who had been learning to say goodbye in the course of dealing with a disruptive marker event in her personal life—realized that the children's behavior signified their unspoken efforts to cauterize their hearts. In the face of the imminent loss of a relationship—and an environment of relationships—in which they had experienced and done together tremendously important growth, they had no words but only actions to express their distress. If they could be angry with her and sullen with each other, perhaps the pain of ending this important time and context of human care and growth could be dealt with. Since that realization, she has learned to begin six weeks before the end of school, helping them to write about, to bring to word, to celebrate, grieve, and then joyfully give up, a shared reality that is about to end. "The end is where we start from."

The symbolic death involved in any significant ending has four interrelated phases, says Bridges. These are disengagement, disidentification, disenchantment, and disorientation.

Disengagement. We experience disengagement whenever we give up a significant connection to some context of relationship and shared meanings that has become important to our sense of self. Extreme experiences of disengagement include deaths, divorces, and the catastrophic destruction of a home and its belongings. Lesser forms come with job changes, moves, illness, the end of a school year, and the like. With disengagement an inexorable process of change begins.

Disidentification. In breaking or losing old connections with the world, we lose important ways of self-definition. Some part of our sense of identity must be given up or changed. To some degree one is no longer quite sure who one is. Being no longer "Madame Justice" or "Professor" or "Susan's husband" or "Mr. President" or "pastor of Grace Church" takes a chunk of some size from the felt substance of our identity. Whether the pain of loss or relinquishment is great or small, we wonder if we will "weigh as much" without that identification and connection as we did with it. Disidentification is the internal side of the disengagement process.

Disenchantment. Endings mean giving up—or enduring the collapse of—some part of our previous constructions of reality. We discover that some valued part of our world is no longer real. Santa Claus is revealed as fiction; we find that parents sometimes lie or are afraid; best friends let us down; a lover proves unfaithful; leaders go corrupt; organizations betray our trust; a guardian angel fails to protect us. Equally painful, we have had to face the fact that we ourselves have not lived up to our images of ourselves or that we have made avoidable mistakes. We have been foolhardy, shortsighted, or dishonest. The lesson of disenchantment begins with the discovery that in order to change—really to change and not just to switch positions—we must realize that some significant part of our old reality was in our head, not out there.

Disorientation. The cumulative impact of the three other dimensions we have looked at adds up to disorientation. We have lost our bearings and familiar moorings. Our maps, charts, plans, and purposes seem now remote and meaningless. We are no longer in them. Our wills feel blocked and stymied. Our energy is diffusely absorbed in trying to grasp what has happened to us. We find ourselves on the edge of what Bridges aptly calls the neutral zone.

The Neutral Zone

The neutral zone bears some resemblance to what St. John of the Cross referred to as the "dark night of the soul." In Bridges's work it refers to a "time out of time" and a place that is "no place." One is dislocated in time and space, and the structures of meaning have been shaken or emptied. In the anthropological literature on rites of passage this corresponds to the time after the ritualized death when one goes into the wilderness to search and wait for a vision-dream. Biblically speaking, it is the forty years in the wilderness with the liberated Hebrews, living day to day on manna and following the pillars of cloud and fire wherever they may lead. Or it is the forty days in the wilderness with Jesus, struggling with the demons of temptation and trying to fathom the meaning of a calling.

Whatever the particular form it takes for us, the crucial thing is not to evade the entry into what for Urban Holmes is the "anti-structure." Our culture knows little of how to prepare us for the attentive waiting of the neutral zone. It is eager to offer us medicines and panaceas, distractions and remedies, to help us avoid the pain of dislocation and the helplessness of suspended movement and direction that the neutral zone imposes. But to bail out, to escape from, or to narcotize ourselves against the neutral zone is to miss the great gift that sojourning in the interstices of the world can give us. In Bridges's perspective the neutral zone represents a fruitful emptiness, a time of return to the primal chaos out of which, alone, new creation can come. The power of the neutral zone for our renewal and eventual return comes from the perspective it provides on the life flow from which we have, temporarily, withdrawn. "Viewed from the emptiness of the neutral zone," Bridges says, "the realities of the everyday world look transparent and insubstantial and we can see what is meant by the statement that everything is 'illusion'. . . . The neutral zone provides an access to an angle of vision on life that one can get nowhere else. And it is a succession of such views over a lifetime that produces wisdom."

The congregation that intends to be an ecology of care and vocation will take seriously the guiding, pacing, and supporting of persons in their times in the neutral zone. Companions who do not panic in the face of aimless waiting or who do not have an obsessive need to clean up messiness can help make time in the neutral zone less lonely. Good guidance and support encourage those in the neutral zone to keep as many of the routine structures of their lives in place as they can. As Carlyle Marney used to say, "You shouldn't rattle *all* the tentpoles in your tepee at the same time." In the midst of the neutral-zone time, however, the pilgrim needs regular time and space to be alone. It is a good time to begin a log of neutral-zone experiences and insights. I learned as a teenage boat captain that you can steer a big boat either by setting its prow on a distant goal or by watching its wake. Keeping a set of daily notations in the neutral zone helps one begin to steer by the wake. The neutral zone can be a good space in one's life to write an autobiography and look at the deeper patterns and movements of one's life. The "Unfolding Tapestry of My Life" work sheet and instructions included in the appendix of this book provide a proven method for approaching the autobiographical task. Time in the neutral zone is important for discovering what one really wants. There is profound wisdom in the spiritual director's suggestion that in this time one meditate on one's deep hungers, or that one contemplate what would be unlived in one's life if it ended today. Part of learning to trust the Spirit of God in our spirit is to trust that what we most deeply and truly yearn for has something profoundly to do with what God wants for us. Of course one may be in therapy or spiritual direction during a neutral-zone time, and that can be an important part of one's listening and attending and of one's waiting and discernment. In either event, it is a time to lay the newness and unknownness, the fright, the fear, and even the guilt, of being in this place, before God. It is crucial that we affirm in this place the trust and hope that the One who made us will in due season disclose the gift of new direction and restored purpose and energy.

New Beginnings

When our time in the neutral zone has done its work; when the methods we have found for listening to the deeper voices of our spirit and the Spirit of God have borne their fruit; when the coiled and twisted parts of our souls or lives that we needed to have healed have been treated—then we are ready to make a new beginning. It is notoriously difficult to give a formula for telling when the work of a deep-going therapy is done. Similarly, there is no general rule or guideline for discerning when the sojourn in interstitial space and time has done its work. But somehow, if we have been faithful to the process, we know. Bridges speaks poetically about this: When we are ready to make a beginning, we shortly will find an opportunity. We are given subtle hints—inner signals that alert us to the proximity of new beginnings. We get faint intimations; we hear a subtle new theme in the music; we catch a strange new fragrance on the breeze, and soon we begin to discern the shape of the next step.

In this stage of new beginnings it is important not to rush things. A comprehensive, gradual reintegration of life in light of the newness that came from the neutral zone must take place. Pastoral care—congregational care—must help persons pace this reentry and reintegration, protecting the fragile new against the power of old patterns or the premature forging of new ones.

As we move now to our next chapter, on the congregation as ecology of care and vocation, let us carry with us a proper appreciation and regard for the depth of upheaval and deconstruction which times of deep-going change require in our lives. And let us honor the time, space, courage, and faith it requires to meet and attend to the spirit of new creation which God means to give us in the neutral-zone times of our lives.

CHAPTER 7

Pastoral Care, Faith Development, Public Church

The central themes of this book go together and require one another. Let us review briefly the thought itinerary of these pages. We have looked at practical theology as the congregation's way of shaping its mission in light both of its memory and hope and of its grasp of the present challenges it is called to engage. In that regard we have examined the qualities of commitment and action that constitute a congregation as a "public church." We have reconsidered vocation, seeing it as the correlative of a covenantal understanding of the church. Building on this interpretation of covenant and vocation, we undertook to think through what it would mean to ground pastoral care in the concern for awakening, shaping, encouraging, correcting, and healing vocation, understood as "finding a purpose for one's life that is part of the purposes of God." In a theologically constructive chapter, we sought to clarify a perspective on the purposes of God and on the human vocation to partnership with God's action and intentions. In that overview we worked with the insight that humans are called as part of nature to be reflective and consciously corresponsible partners in God's creation. This led to our elaborating a developmental theory of how humans become conscious and critically aware subjects before God and with one another.

Building on these theoretical perspectives, we turned again to the congregation, viewing it as an ecology of developmental presences. There we began the process of thinking through how pastoral care can meet persons at their various stages of development and support the deepening of vocation. Throughout we have tried to build on our theme of seeing the congregation as covenant community, and seeing pastoral care as the formation of the congregation as an ecology of care and vocation in a public church.

The last chapter explored some of the dynamics of personal change. With this, and with all that went before, we have prepared the way for some thoughts on how a practical theology of pastoral care can strengthen the congregation's effectiveness as an ecology of care and vocation in the movement toward being a public church.

THE CRUCIAL ROLE OF PASTORAL LEADERSHIP

Before we turn toward the practical directions that flow from this itinerary of reflection, I must say a word about the critical importance of pastoral leadership if the ideas of lay vocation, faith development, and the public church are to get anywhere at all. In a course I teach on education and pastoral care for a public church, students have recently done in-depth studies of the patterns of leadership and dynamics of community life in a variety of Atlanta congregations that we identified as public churches. Our studies confirmed what had already become clear in the empirical research on public churches included in the important work of Roozen, McKinney, and Carroll:[1] in the development and continuing vitality of public-church communities the role of effective and committed pastoral leadership is fundamental. Pastors, priests, and other professional leaders in the community cannot create a public church commitment by themselves: the studies make this very clear. But it is clearly a necessary, if not sufficient, condition for the forming and sustaining of a public-church community that there be an imaginative and generative pastoral leadership.

We also found, as did Roozen, McKinney, and Carroll, that the pastoral leadership and the patterns of lay leadership that joined with it must balance the channeling of energy they commit to the empowering and supporting of the laity in their public vocations, with an equal attention to the nurture and healing of persons in their spiritual development. Pastoral leadership and the ecology of care and vocation it seeks to form must attend both to the nurturing of public presence and vocations and to the nurturing and supporting of souls in their personal pilgrimages of faith.

Without exception, the pastoral leaders we have studied in public churches have an authority that issues from their trust in, and ability to empower and support, strong patterns of lay leadership and initiative. The forming and strengthening of an ecology of care and vocation calls for "sharing the *praxis*." It calls for patterns of care that empower the congregation in doing its practical theology, and for theological leaders who find joy in opening access for members to the sources and resources of faith.

CARE AND SPONSORSHIP

Development in faith and selfhood comes through the work of God's spirit in us. It also comes as the fruit of meeting experiences of critical challenge in our lives in interplay with the interpretive resources of the Christian story and the support and encouragement of the community of faith. Provision for this interplay I call a "community of sponsorship." The idea of a sponsor comes from the early church where a convert and candidate for baptism had a sponsor to guide him or her through the one-to-three-year process of conversion and formation in the catechumenate. A sponsor is one who has gone before us. He or she knows the terrain we must enter into. The sponsor and sponsoring community have maps and models to offer pilgrims. They know how to walk alongside, to encourage, and to help pace the movement of the pilgrim.

A community of sponsorship provides what Bob Kegan has called a "holding environment"[2]—a safe space in which persons can do the important though sometimes frightening and difficult work of deconstruction and reconstruction. Here some of the insights from the previous chapter can be helpful, as well as the important work of Evelyn Whitehead and James Whitehead[3] on the ways communities of faith can pace and support persons in times of deep-going crisis and change. A crucial contribution that the congregation, in its provision of holding environments, can offer is to "re-cognize" us as we undergo difficult times of healing or transformation.[4] In the midst of deep-going change or conversion we need both confirmations of continuity with contexts and relations that are essential to us, and confirmations in the newness and change being worked in us. The "re-cognition" of a congregational holding environment can be crucial in this regard. Through the appropriate use of developmental theories, it is possible to give persons images to understand what they are undergoing, and to help them avoid panic or premature foreclosure of a developmental transition.[5]

But a community of sponsorship also offers theological resources. It offers stories and images by which persons can make sense of what they are undergoing in light of the Christian memory and hope. It provides disciplines and guidance in prayer and in the contemplative study of Scripture.[6] It promises and supports persons in the trust that the Spirit of God works with our spirits as we seek to ground our lives more deeply in response to the call of God to partnership.

Obviously an important task of pastoral leadership in the congregation is to call forth, prepare, and support teams of persons to serve as sponsoring partners and communities for those engaged in the deepening of vocations and faith. In the next section some of the elements of that preparation and support and some tools and occasions for sponsorship will be offered.

THE CONGREGATION AS AN ENVIRONMENT OF DEVELOPMENTAL EXPECTATION

It is worth pausing a moment to reflect on the ethos of the congregations we know best. What images of the course of adult faith and selfhood do they project? To what conceptions of religious experience and salvation do they overtly and covertly call people? What do the architecture and furniture, the art and decor, of the places of worship and assembly communicate about the dynamics and direction of faith and vocation in the Christian life? What conclusions might a thoughtful person reach about the attitudes toward change in our congregations, based on careful listening to and observation of our liturgies, our prayers, our sermons, and our hymns?

What I am really asking is that we begin an inventory that will help us see whether, or to what degree, our congregations constitute "environments of developmental expectation." Do we signal that ongoing growth and change in faith and vocation are expected and will be supported? Do we provide images and understandings that will sponsor persons in moving into the questions and issues that seem to lie on the frontiers of their commitments in faith and vocation? Do we draw on the rich process imagery our tradition offers in the themes of journey, pilgrimage, wilderness, shipwreck, struggle, rescue, growth from being milkeaters to being meateaters, healing, the new being in Christ, and the promised land?

There are a number of ways we can intentionally evolve toward strengthening the congregation as an environment of developmental expectation and support. First, in our preaching and teaching we can offer dynamic images of faith and calling. These do not, to be sure, have to be the overt content of all our sermons and curricula. Nonetheless, a sermon series exploring images of growth in faith from the New Testament, or on biblical images of calling, liberation, journey, and pilgrimage, can be exciting.[7] If one is careful to avoid preaching people into the trap of individual self-actualization as the goal of development, it is possible to share, in sermon and teaching, adaptations of life-span or adult developmental theories in dialogue with the Christian story and vision.[8] My real point is that we should try to become conscious of the images of the Christian life, salvation, vocation, and redemption which enter into our preaching, prayers, liturgical planning,[9] and pastoral counseling. Subtly and gradually, but pervasively, we can help to form an ethos and language of developmental expectation and support in the congregation that will be energizing.

Second, building on the pioneering work of John Westerhoff and Will Willimon on liturgy and the life cycle,[10] we can begin to develop and offer liturgical celebrations of rites of passage in the life cycle and in the development of faith and vocation. Although it is not possible here to spell out this proposal in detail, we should rethink confirmation in the light of faith development theory. Increasingly we should view it as a time for recognizing the young person's assumption of responsibility for the baptismal vows the parents earlier made. It should be an occasion for celebrating the young person's new intentionality in deepening her relationship with God in Christ, in embracing full membership in the people of God, and in building on the awakening and shaping of vocation in and beyond the community. The covenant community, in response, should confirm its trust and support of the youth in his quest for deepened faith and the forming of vocation and should confirm its anticipation of celebration when the young adult is ready in the community to declare how he is finding a purpose for his life that is part of the purposes of God.

There could also be important liturgical celebrations or observances of other critical times or passages in our lives. There should be a time for young adults in their twenties or thirties to share with the congregation their vocational directions. This should come when one or more of the young adults in the community are ready for it. It can be a tremendously significant time in the common life of the community and the young adults to receive the evidence of the Spirit's work in their lives and to make their personal covenants with God part of the covenant of the community of faith. Such a rite would truly be the culmination and completion of the promises of their confirmation. Similarly, we should consider developing liturgical celebrations of the regrounding and renewal of vocation as part of persons' completing a midlife transition or as they begin retirement.[11]

Third, as a basis for discerning and supporting the movement toward renewal and regrounding of vocation at various points in the adult pilgrimage, I propose that we begin to offer periodic faith development and vocation inventories or checkups. Such an opportunity can be offered to new members who come to the community by transfer or by profession of faith as a part of their preparation for membership in this particular congregation of the Christian church. Often we treat too lightly the faith biographies of persons who join the church as adults. When we do so we fail to tap into, and help them bring to word, the hungers or new resolves they bring in their hopes for their belonging to this new community. Opportunities for faith and vocation self-inventory can also be offered regularly in a retreat or spiritual-direction format for individuals or groups of adults who are already members.

In the appendix of this book one can find the instructions and work sheet for what we call "The Unfolding Tapestry of My Life." It is a carefully designed and tested instrument for use with persons from middle adolescence on through adulthood, to lead them in a careful and deep autobiographical reflection. If used properly, this is a powerful tool. It has been developed at the Center for Faith Development from work with the journal-workshop methods of Ira Progroff, the insights of *The Spiritual Exercises of St. Ignatius,* the ideas of Daniel Levinson, and the application of faith development theory. Persons should be given an extended time for completing the steps of the Tapestry (minimum, three hours). Their work should be for themselves alone. (If we anticipate sharing something like this in detail with others, we are inevitably less honest than we can be when we are doing it for ourselves and God alone.) It is of crucial importance, however, that persons given the Tapestry should also be given opportunities with the pastor, or with the pastoral care team or peers, to share the learnings, insights, questions, and determinations they make in the course of working with the Tapestry. Pastors who choose to use it should provide for careful processing of the experiences people have with the Tapestry. Frequently it helps people name and recognize their need to work with times of pain or breakthrough in their lives which there has been no previous opportunity to address. Pastors and pastoral teams who consider using the Tapestry should work with it fully themselves and evaluate their experiences before deciding to use it with others.

Fourth, pastoral care in a congregation of the public church will make it a principal concern to provide contexts and help for the healing of the disjunctions people experience between their work and life in the techno-economic order and their public roles, on the one hand, and their private lives in family, church, and leisure activities, on the other. The "disjunction of realms" of which Daniel Bell speaks constitutes a serious set of obstacles to vocational integrity and to the integrity of a public church.[12] Provision for lay practical theologians to study, reflect, pray, and struggle together about how to shape their occupations and workplaces in vocational directions is essential for care and vocation in a public church.

Finally, pastoral care for a public church needs to provide for persons to come to terms with the stranger, in the several senses we have used the word here: the stranger within, in terms of the hidden movements of the Spirit in our lives and our unconscious dimensions; the strangers who are our companions in covenant community; the stranger who is Jesus Christ, the liberator, redeemer, and enactor of the in-breaking kingdom of God; and the strangers who are our brothers and sisters in the public of our pluralistic communities and our global city.[13] It is part of the pastoral care of public churches that we offer hospitality to the stranger who is a political victim or religious refugee. It is pastoral therapy for satiated—or saturated—souls that we enter into solidarity with those who are homeless and defeated in our competitive society.

THEOLOGICAL REGROUNDING
AND THE RECOVERY OF
ESCHATOLOGY

The overall thrust of this book is in the direction of a regrounding of practical theology. At the center of the book's position is the effort to direct our attention to the *praxis* of God as the unified and yet infinitely multiplex larger action of which we are a part. The vocation of the church, and the vocation of Christians, is to align our efforts as responsible selves, as much as we can, with the purposes and work of God. To take this seriously is to embrace the direction of being and becoming a public church. Faith development theory, in league with a theory of the developing self, has a role to play in this kind of practical theology. It provides a descriptive and normative framework for guiding a pastoral care aimed at supporting and challenging persons toward being critically aware subjects before God and in partnership with God and the neighbor.

In a real sense all of this depends on whether we trust and see a God at work in the universe and in our histories with whom we can make covenant and serve. Radically to trust that God intends and is active toward the realization of a kingdom of God that already breaks into our present with redeeming and liberating power is to experience a subtle but powerful reversal in our sense of time. Common-sensically, we all learned that the present and future comes to us out of the past. What happened yesterday has shaped what happens today; what happens today will determine the shape of things tomorrow. But with Jesus' pointing to the in-breaking future of God's kingdom and to God's intended fulfillment of creation as the power of the future, we find ourselves grounded in time in a fundamentally new way. We begin to see that newness, possibility, and freedom come to us in each moment from God's future, as the gift of divine grace. We begin to see God as active in ongoing creation, governance, and liberation and redemption, luring and conserving creation toward God's future. And in renewed and sustained hope we turn toward the neighbor and stranger, and the encompassing systems of our common lives, with refreshed vision and purpose and with regrounded faith and vocation.

The Unfolding Tapestry of My Life

INSTRUCTIONS FOR THE RESPONDENT

Take a moment to look over the work sheet on pages 124-25. After you have looked at the chart for a few minutes, turn back to this page for some explanation of the categories at the top of the work sheet.

1. *Calendar years from birth.* Starting at the left column of the work sheet, number down the column from the year of your birth to the present year. If there are a substantial number of years in your life, you may wish to number the columns in two-year intervals.

2. *Place—geographic and socioeconomic.* Here you may record your sense of place in several different ways. It could be the physical place you lived in at different times in your life, including the geographic area where you lived, or it could be your sense of your position in society or in the community. Record your sense of place in whatever way seems most appropriate to you.

3. *Key relationships.* These can be any types of relationships that you feel had a significant impact on your life at the time. The persons mentioned need not be living now, and you need not have known them personally. (That is, they could be persons who influenced you through your reading or hearing about them, etc.)

4. *Uses and directions of the self.* Here you can record not only how you spent your time but also what you thought you were doing at that time.

5. *Marker events.* Here you may record the events that you remember which marked turning points in your life—moves, marriages, divorces, etc. Major events occur, and things are never the same again.

6. *Age by year.* This column simply gives you another chronological point of reference. Fill it in with the same intervals you used for calendar years on the left-hand side of the chart.

7. *Events and conditions in society.* In this column we ask you to record what you remember of what was going on in the world at various times in your life. Record this as an image or phrase, or a series of images and phrases, that best sums up the period for you.

8. *Images of God.* This is an invitation for you to record briefly, in a phrase or two, what your thoughts or images of God—positive and negative—were at different times of your life. If you had no image of God or cannot remember one, answer appropriately.

9. *Centers of value and power.* What persons, objects, institutions, or goals formed a center for your life at this time? What attracted you, what

repelled you, what did you commit your time and energy to, and what did you choose to avoid? Record only the one or two most important ones.

10. *Authorities.* This column asks to whom or what you looked for guidance or to ratify your decisions and choices at various points in your life.

As you work on the chart, make brief notes to yourself indicating the thoughts you have under each of the columns. It is not necessary to fill out the columns in great detail. You are doing the exercise for yourself, so use shorthand or brief notes.

After you have finished your work with the chart, spend some time thinking about your life as a whole. Try to feel its movement and its flow, its continuities and discontinuities. As you look at the Tapestry, let yourself imagine your life a drama or a play. Where would the divisions of it naturally fall? If you were to divide it into chapters or episodes, how would these be titled? When you have a sense of how your life might be divided, draw lines through these areas on the chart and jot down the titles on the reverse side of the work sheet.

This is the unfolding tapestry of your life at this particular time. In the coming days or months you may want to return to it for further reflection or to add things that may come to you later. Some people find that the Tapestry exercise is a good beginning for keeping a regular journal or diary. You may find, too, that if you come back to this exercise after some time has passed, the chapters and titles in your life will be different as you look at them in the light of new experiences.

Work Sheet

The Unfolding Tapestry of My Life

Calendar years from birth	Place— geographic and socioeconomic	Key relationships	Uses and directions of the self	Marker events

The Unfolding Tapestry of My Life

Age by year	Events and conditions in society	Images of God	Centers of value and power	Authorities

Notes

CHAPTER 1

1. A brief statement of this account is in Edward Farley, "Theology and Practice Outside the Clerical Paradigm," in *Practical Theology: The Emerging Field in Theology, Church, and World,* Don S. Browning (New York: Harper & Row, 1983), 21–41. The longer statement of Farley's position is in Farley, *Theologia: The Fragmentation and Unity of Theological Education* (Philadelphia: Fortress Press,1983).

2. On the concept of *praxis* and its history, see Nicholas Lobkowitz, *Theory and Practice: The History of a Marxist Concept, from Aristotle to Marx* (Notre Dame, Ind.: Univ. of Notre Dame Press, 1967), and Richard J. Bernstein, *Praxis and Action* (Philadelphia: Univ. of Pennsylvania Press, 1971).

3. For an excellent discussion of the classical Greek virtues as they have been "converted" into Christian ethics, see Josef Pieper, *The Four Cardinal Virtues* (Notre Dame, Ind.: Univ. of Notre Dame Press, 1966 [1954]).

4. For a helpful description of these three orientations of knowing in Aristotle, see Thomas H. Groome, *Christian Religious Education: A Shared Praxis Approach* (New York: Harper & Row, 1980), 153–157.

5. See Bernstein, *Praxis and Action,* 42–76.

6. For this characterization and its background, see James W. Fowler, "Practical Theology and the Shaping of Christian Lives," in *Practical Theology,* ed. Browning, idem, 149ff.; and "Practical Theology and Theological Education," *Theology Today* 42 (1985): 49ff.

7. For earlier depictions of the charts to be given here, see the two articles cited in 6.

8. See David Tracy, "The Foundations of Practical Theology, in ed. Browning, *Practical Theology,* 62–63.

9. Søren Kierkegaard, *Purity of Heart,* trans. Douglas V. Steere (New York: Harper & Bros., 1938), 180–81.

10. Charles V. Gerkin, *The Living Human Document* (Nashville: Abingdon Press, 1984), chap. 8.

11. Richard Sennett, *The Fall of Public Man* (New York: Alfred A. Knopf, 1976).

12. Ibid., 337–40.

13. Martin E. Marty, *The Public Church* (New York: Crossroad, 1981).

14. Parker J. Palmer, *The Company of Strangers* (New York: Crossroad, 1983).

15. The phrase is that of Carl Michaelson, my teacher of systematics at Drew Theological Seminary, who died untimely in 1965. See his book *The Hinge of History* (New York: Charles Scribner's Sons, 1959).

CHAPTER 2

1. Walter Brueggemann, "Covenanting as Human Vocation," *Interpretation* 33 (1979); 115–129.

2. Karl Holl, "The History of the Word Vocation (Beruf)", trans. Heber F. Peacock (unpub.), ET of Holl, "Die Geschichte des Worts Beruf," in *Gesammelte Aufsatze zur Kirchengeschichte*, vol. 3 (Tübingen: J. C. B. Mohr [Paul Siebeck], 1928), 189–219.

3. Arthur E. Lovejoy, *The Great Chain of Being* (1936; reprint, New York: Harper & Row, Torchbooks, 1960).

4. Holl, "History," 6. The reason that medical people are at the bottom of the medieval hierarchy lies in the fact that they must deal with the body, body fluids, and corporeal materiality, which are at the other end of the great chain from spiritual reality.

5. Frederick Buechner, *Wishful Thinking: A Theological ABC* (New York: Harper & Row, 1973), 95.

6. See James W. Fowler, *Becoming Adult, Becoming Christian* (New York: Harper & Row, 1984), esp. chap. 4.

7. See Joseph Allen, *Love and Conflict: A Covenantal Model of Christian Ethics* (Nashville: Abingdon Press, 1984). For a discussion of covenant, organism, and contract as root metaphors, see James W. Fowler, "Pluralism, Particularity, and Paideia," *Journal of Law and Religion* 2 (1984): 268–69, 300–305.

8. The phrase "mystery-mastery" is that of David Bakan in *The Duality of Human Existence* (Boston: Beacon Press, 1966). It refers to a tendency to hide the sources of one's knowledge or authority for the sake of keeping those whom one leads or dominates in a position of dependence.

9. This language for clarifying the meaning of covenant I owe to H. Richard Niebuhr and Josiah Royce. See Niebuhr, *Radical Monotheism and Western Culture* (New York: Harper & Bros., 1960), and Royce, *The Philosophy of Loyalty* (New York: Macmillan Co., 1908).

CHAPTER 3

1. For a summary account and analysis of Niebuhr's treatment of these metaphors, see James W. Fowler, *To See The Kingdom: The Theological Vision of H. Richard Niebuhr* (Lanham, Md.: Press of America, 1985 [1974]), 134–200.

2. Jürgen Moltmann, *God in Creation: A New Theology of Creation and The Spirit of God* trans. Margaret Kohl (New York: Harper & Row,1985).

3. Langdon Gilkey, *Reaping the Whirlwind: A Christian Interpretation of History* (New York: Seabury Press, 1976).

4. James Weldon Johnson, *God's Trombones* (New York: Viking Press, 1927), 17–20. The quotes given here come from "The Creation."

5. Moltmann, *God in Creation.*

6. Paul Davies, *Superforce: The Search of a Grand Unified Theory of Nature* (New York: Simon & Schuster, 1984), 16.

7. Ibid., 10–11.

8. I acknowledge with gratitude the influence on ideas and formulations in this section, of Gilkey's careful efforts at reconstruction of a contemporary Christian doctrine of providence in *Reaping the Whirlwind.*

9. Martin Buber, *The Knowledge of Man* (New York: Harper & Row, Torchbooks, 1965), 127.

10. Simone Weil, *Waiting for God* (New York: Harper & Bros., Colophon Books, 1951). See there "The Love of God and Affliction," 117ff.

CHAPTER 4

1. On Piaget's work, see Jean Piaget, "Piaget's Theory," in *Carmichael's Manual of Child Psychology,* 3d ed., vol. 1, ed. Paul Mussen (New York: John Wiley & Sons, 1970), 703–732; and idem, *Six Psychological Studies* (New York: Random House, 1967). On Piaget, see Herbert Ginsberg and Sylvia Opper, *Piaget's Theory of Intellectual Development* (Englewood Cliffs, N.J.: Prentice-Hall, 1969).

2. Lawrence Kohlberg, *Essays on Moral Development,* vols. 1 and 2 (New York: Harper & Row, 1981–84). On Kohlberg and Piaget, see James W. Fowler, *Stages of Faith* (New York: Harper & Row, 1981) 41–86.

3. Robert L. Selman, *The Growth of Interpersonal Understanding* (New York: Academic Press, 1980).

4. James W. Fowler, *Stages of Faith,* 119–213; idem, *Becoming Adult, Becoming Christian* (New York: Harper & Row, 1984), chap. 3; idem (with Jerome Berryman and Sam Keen), *Life-Maps: Conversations on the Journey of Faith,* 2d ed. (Waco, Tex.: Word Books, 1985), 14–101; and idem, "Faith and the Structuring of Meaning," in *Toward Moral and Religious Maturity,* ed. Christianne Brusselmans, James W. Fowler, and Antoine Vergote (Morristown, N.J.: Silver Burdett Co., 1980), 51–85.

5. Robert Kegan, *The Evolving Self: Problems and Process in Human Development* (Cambridge: Harvard Univ. Press, 1982), and idem, "There the Dance Is: Religious Dimensions of a Developmental Framework," in *Toward Moral and Religious Maturity,* ed. Brusselmans et al., 403–40.

6. Steven Sawyer Ivy, *"The Structural-Developmental Theories of James Fowler and Robert Kegan as Resources for Pastoral Assessment"* (Diss. Southeran Baptist Theol. Sem. 1985).

7. For characterizations of the way I use the term "faith" see Fowler, *Stages of Faith,* xi–36, 91–97, 274–86; idem, *Becoming Adult, Becoming Christian,* 50–52; idem, "Faith and the Structuring of Meaning," 53–64; and idem, "Pluralism, Particularity, and Paideia," *Journal of Law and Religion* 2 (1984); 292–96.

8. See esp. Erik H. Erikson, *Identity, Youth, and Crisis* (New York: W. W. Norton & Co., 1968).

9. David Riesman, with Nathan Glazer and Reuel Denney, *The Lonely Crowd: A Study of the Changing American Character* (New Haven: Yale Univ. Press, 1950).

10. Paul Ricoeur, *The Symbolism of Evil*, trans. Emerson Buchanan (Boston: Beacon Press, 1967), 351-52; idem, "The Hermeneutics of Symbols and Philosophical Reflection," in *The Philosophy of Paul Ricoeur*, ed. Charles E. Reagan and David Stewart (Boston: Beacon Press, 1978), 36-58.

CHAPTER 5

1. Carl Schneider, "Faith Development and Pastoral Diagnosis," in *Faith Development and Fowler*, ed. Craig Dykstra and Sharon L. Parks (Birmingham, Ala.: Religious Education Press, 1986).

2. Steven Sawyer Ivy, "The Structural-Development Theories of James Fowler and Robert Kegan as Resources for Pastoral Assessment" (Diss., Southern Baptist Theol. Sem., 1985).

3. Jerome Berryman, "Being in Parables with Children," *Religious Education* 74 (1979): 271-85.

4. Bruno Bettelheim, *The Uses of Enchantment: The Meaning and Importance of Fairy Tales* (New York: Random House, Vintage Books, 1977).

5. On the impact of television and other media on contemporary children, see Thomas Lickona, *Raising Good Children* (New York: Bantam Books, 1983), 350-65; and David Elkind, *The Hurried Child (Reading, Mass.: Addison-Wesley, 1981), 71-94*.

6. See David Heller, "The Children's God," *Psychology Today* 19 (1985); 22-27. In book form, see David Heller, *The Children's God* (Chicago: Univ. of Chicago Press, 1986).

7. See Alfred Messer, "Father Hunger," *Journal of the Medical Association of Georgia* 74 (1985): 822-24.

8. For the most helpful discussion of the transition from the Synthetic-Conventional to the Individuative-Reflective stage, and of young adult faith, see Sharon Parks, *The Critical Years; The Young Adult Search for a Faith to Live By* (New York: Harper & Row, 1986).

9. Ronald Marstin, *Beyond Our Tribal Gods: The Maturing of Faith* (Maryknoll, N.Y.: Orbis Books, 1979).

10. See James W. Fowler, *Stages of Faith: The Psychology of Human Development and the Quest for Meaning* (New York: Harper & Row 1981), 106-14.

11. See the important discussion of these issues in Philip M. Helfaer, *The Psychology of Religious Doubt* (Boston: Beacon Press, 1972), esp. part 2, "Faith and Doubt in the Precocious Identity Formation," 63-89.

12. Kenneth Kenniston, "Psychological Development and Historical Change," in *Explorations in Psychohistory, ed. Robert Jay Lifton (New York: Simon and Schuster, 1974), 160-164*.

CHAPTER 6

1. J. McKim Malville, *The Fermenting Universe* (New York: Seabury Press, 1974), 2-3.

2. I have found two books especially helpful in this regard. The first, which is

not specifically addressed to pastors or ecclesial care, is Peter Marris, *Loss and Change* (New York: Pantheon Books, 1974). The second is directly addressed to the Christian community: Evelyn E. Whitehead and James D. Whitehead, *Christian Life Patterns: The Psychological Challenges and Religious Invitations of Adult Life* (Garden City, N.Y.: Doubleday & Co., 1979).

3. William Bridges, *Transitions: Making Sense of Life's Changes* (Reading, Mass.: Addison-Wesley, 1980).

CHAPTER 7

1. David A. Roozen, William McKinney, and Jackson W. Carroll, *Varieties of Religious Presence: Mission in Public Life* (New York: Pilgrim Press, 1984). The members of my class who conducted the studies of public churches in Atlanta include Tahti Amuuru, Victor Casad, Lora Groton, Susan McAllan, Bonnie Roddy, and Anne Salter. The Reverend Fred Smith was graduate assistant in the course. Bishop Neville DeSouza was an active auditing member of the course.

2. See Robert Kegan, *The Evolving Self* (Cambridge: Harvard Univ. Press, 1982), 256ff.

3. See Evelyn Eaton Whitehead and James D. Whitehead, *Christian Life Patterns: The Psychological Challenges and Religious Invitations of Adult Life* (New York: Doubleday & Co., 1979), esp. chaps. 1 and 2.

4. Robert Kegan, "There The Dance Is: Religious Dimensions of a Developmental Framework," in *Toward Moral and Religious Maturity,* ed. Christianne Brusselmans, James W. Fowler, and Antoine Vergote (Morristown, N.J.: Silver Burdett Co., 1980), 426.

5. See Whitehead and Whitehead, *Christian Life Patterns,* 56–70.

6. See Richard J. Foster, *Celebration of Discipline* (New York: Harper & Row, 1978); Walter Brueggemann, *Praying the Psalms* (Winona, Minn.: St. Mary's Press, 1982); Matthew Fox, *Original Blessing* (Santa Fe, N. Mex.: Bear & Co., 1983); Ernest Boyer, Jr., *A Way in the World: Family Life as Spiritual Discipline* (New York: Harper & Row, 1984); and Don E. Saliers, *The Soul in Paraphrase* (New York: Crossroad-Seabury, 1980).

7. See William J. Bouwsma, "Christian Adulthood," in *Adulthood,* ed. Erik H. Erikson (New York: W. W. Norton & Co., 1978), 81–96; Daniel Jenkins, *Christian Maturity and Christian Success* (Philadelphia: Fortress Press, 1982); Paul Van Buren, *Discerning the Way* (New York: Seabury Press, 1980); and Evelyn Eaton Whitehead and James D. Whitehead, *Seasons of Strength: New Visions of Adult Christian Maturing* (New York: Doubleday & Co., 1984).

8. This was the principal aim of my book *Becoming Adult, Becoming Christian* (New York: Harper & Row, 1984).

9. See William H. Willimon, *Worship as Pastoral Care* (Nashville: Abingdon Press, 1975), and Robert L. Browning and Roy A. Reed, *The Sacraments in Religious Education and Liturgy* (Birmingham, Ala.: Religious Education Press, 1985).

10. John H. Westerhoff and William H. Willimon, *Liturgy and Learning Through the Life Cycle* (New York: Seabury Press, 1980).

11. The pervasive individualism that is normative in this society, and in our

churches, makes any public celebration of the experience of renewal after a time of struggle in midlife seem threatening. If however, we should develop a program of regular times of self- and pastoral-assessment, and the provision of retreats or extended-weekly-meeting formats for dealing with spiritual and vocational renewal at appropriate points in adulthood, such celebrations should come quite naturally. They should be a source of encouragement to peers and younger adults. In connection with preparation for vocational renewal at retirement, it should be noted that we are now seeing the emergence of the first true leisure class in history on a large scale—men and women of retirement age who have ten to fifteen years of good health expectancy and reasonable financial resources. They, more freely than anyone else, have leeway to shape vocations that combine service and contribution with a rhythm and pace that suit them. The congregation can do a great deal to help in the anticipation of retirement and the shaping of postretirement vocations.

12. Daniel Bell, *The Cultural Contradictions of Capitalism* (New York: Basic Books, 1978), xx–xxi, 146–171.

13. See Parker J. Palmer, *The Company of Strangers* (New York: Crossroads, 1981), and Thomas Ogletree, *Hospitality to Strangers* (Philadelphia: Fortress Press, 1985).

Printed in the United States
22892LVS00001B/382-534

9 780800 617394